KT-548-523

DISCARDED

FROM

RICHMOND UPON THAMES

LIBRARY SERVICE

30p

USER'S GUIDE
TO THE BIBLE

Copyright © 1984 Lion Publishing

Published by
Lion Publishing
Icknield Way, Tring, Herts, England
ISBN 0 85648 409 1
Lion Publishing Corporation
10885 Textile Road, Belleville, Michigan 48111 , USA
ISBN 0 85648 409 1
Albatross Books
PO Box 320, Sutherland, NSW 2232, Australia
ISBN 0 86760 474 3

Quotations, used by kind permission,
from the *Good News Bible*,
copyright 1966, 1971 and 1976
American Bible Society,
published by Bible Societies/Collins
New International Version,
copyright 1978 New York Bible Society

First edition 1984
Phototypesetting by Parkway Group,
London and Abingdon
Printed in Yugoslavia
by Mladinska Knjiga Printing House

The photographs in this book have been
supplied by ZEFA.

Additional photographs are reproduced by
permission of the following photographers and
agencies:

All-Sport Photographic 52, 44–45
Barnaby's Picture Library 10–11, 89
Bay Picture Library 49
John Cleare Mountain Camera 2–3
Colour Library International 103
Sonia Halliday Photographs/Sister Daniel 121/
    Sonia Halliday 58–59, 109, 123
Robert Harding Picture Library/G. P. Lewis
    106–107
Alan Hutchison 51, 69, 117
Lion Publishing 54, 125/Simon Jenkins 6,
    16/Jon Willcocks 14–15, 18, 19, 20–21, 46,
    61, 65, 66, 88, 110/David Vesey 36
Mansell Collection 97
Picturepoint London 72–73
Popperfoto 24, 25, 39
Rex Features 60
Doug Sewell 22–23, 81
Tony Waltham 103

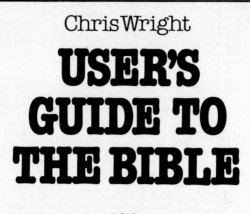

Chris Wright

USER'S GUIDE TO THE BIBLE

A LION MANUAL

BOOKS OF THE OLD TESTAMENT

1

GENESIS

2

EXODUS   DEUTERONOMY
LEVITICUS   JOSHUA
NUMBERS

3

JUDGES

4

1 SAMUEL
2 SAMUEL
1 KINGS

5

1 KINGS   2 CHRONICLES   HOSEA
2 KINGS   ISAIAH   AMOS
1 CHRONICLES   JEREMIAH

6

EZRA   EZEKIEL   MALACHI
NEHEMIAH   HAGGAI
ISAIAH   ZECHARIAH

7

BOOKS OF THE NEW TESTAMENT

8

MATTHEW
MARK
LUKE

9

MATTHEW   JOHN
MARK
LUKE

10

ACTS

11

ROMANS   PHILIPPIANS   TITUS   1 JOHN
1 & 2 CORINTHIANS   COLOSSIANS   HEBREWS   REVELATION
GALATIANS   1 THESSALONIANS   JAMES
EPHESIANS   1 & 2 TIMOTHY   1 PETER

12

USER'S GUIDE

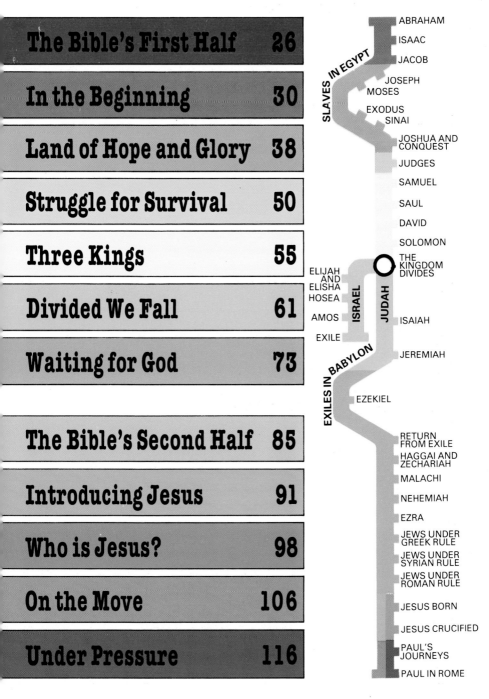

ABRAHAM
ISAAC
JACOB
SLAVES IN EGYPT
JOSEPH
MOSES
EXODUS
SINAI
JOSHUA AND CONQUEST
JUDGES
SAMUEL
SAUL
DAVID
SOLOMON
THE KINGDOM DIVIDES
ELIJAH AND ELISHA
HOSEA
AMOS
EXILE
ISRAEL
JUDAH
ISAIAH
EXILES IN BABYLON
JEREMIAH
EZEKIEL
RETURN FROM EXILE
HAGGAI AND ZECHARIAH
MALACHI
NEHEMIAH
EZRA
JEWS UNDER GREEK RULE
JEWS UNDER SYRIAN RULE
JEWS UNDER ROMAN RULE
JESUS BORN
JESUS CRUCIFIED
PAUL'S JOURNEYS
PAUL IN ROME

INTRODUCTION
How to use this book

The Bible is a big book that bursts with life. It's exciting reading by any standards. In it there are heroes, villains, love songs, assassinations, questions about life and death, and people who make the same sort of mistakes we do. But the Bible is more than just exciting reading. By opening it up we can learn more about the God who made us, and about Jesus, who came to give us a fresh start.

User's Guide to the Bible is for people who want to get started in the Bible. It takes us on a guided tour of the Bible from beginning to end, starting at the book of Genesis. It introduces the main characters, explains what was happening, and shows what the book has to say to us today. It helps us get to grips with the Bible for ourselves.

A quick look inside the Bible shows that it is actually a collection of 66 books, some long, some short. To make it easier to find the way round, each book is split into chapters and verses. In this manual the usual shorthand method has been used to refer to Bible passages. Take 1 Samuel 9:1–27, for example:

The contents page of the **User's Guide** tells you more than just the page numbers for each chapter. It also includes a diagram of the Bible's story, and it lets you know which Bible books are covered by each section of the manual. You can use it like a road atlas if you feel lost.

The **User's Guide** also contains blue boxes which list Bible passages and where to find them. The manual has been designed for use alongside the Bible, rather than on its own. So reading the Bible passages will help you begin to explore the Bible on your own.

For many people the Bible is the most important book they have read. The **User's Guide to the Bible** has been produced for people who want to know what the Bible has to say to them today.

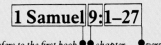

1 Samuel 9:1–27

this refers to the first book ● ● *chapter* ● *verses*
of Samuel (there are 2 of   *number 9*   *1 to 27*
them)

WHAT IS THE BIBLE?

The Bible communicates to us a picture of God. It lets us see and hear what he is like, what he has done, and what he expects of us. Of course there is far more to God than we could ever take in. We do not even understand all there is to know about ourselves – let alone all there is to know about God!

However, the Bible shows us that God did not want to be cloaked in mystery as an unknown and unknowable God. Instead, it seems that he enjoys letting us know about him. He does so in many different ways.

● **Nature.** When we look at the universe as God's creation, we can see something of God's immense power, intelligence and glory.

● **Experience.** Sometimes God communicates directly to us through our own experiences.

● **Jesus Christ.** The best picture God has given us of himself is in the life and words of Jesus. Jesus was God living as a man, and by looking at him we can understand and know God for ourselves.

● **The Bible.** The Bible is an important way in which God communicates to us. It gives us a detailed view of God himself, the world we live in, and of ourselves.

Obviously, the Bible does not contain all there is to know about the world and ourselves. God has given us the gift of curiosity and discovery, and there is plenty that we can find out for ourselves. But in the Bible, God has shown us what we need to know in order to enjoy a close relationship with him.

HOW DID GOD SPEAK?

God spoke in the Bible through people – human beings like ourselves.

He arranged it so that what certain men and women said and wrote down was what he wanted to be said at that time. And he saw to it that when their writings were edited and collected into what we now have as our Bible (a process that went on over a very long time), they continued to be what God wanted to say to people in later generations.

So the Bible is, at the same time, words of men and words of God.
● It was spoken and written by people, using their own minds, mouths and pens.
● But it also came from the mind and will of God, so that what people said and wrote were also the words of God.

This was how some writers in the Bible saw it. They described it as God putting his words into their mouths. Moses told the Israelites that God would send a leader like himself, and God promised: 'I will put my words in his mouth, and he will tell them everything I command him' (Deuteronomy 18:18).

So according to the people who wrote in the Bible, their writings were inspired by God. That does not mean what we sometimes mean by 'inspiration' – that they are full of bright new ideas and clever thoughts. It simply means that they were 'breathed' by God, even as they were being written by men.

Paul sums up not only how the Bible came into existence, but also the reason for using it: 'All Scripture is inspired by God and is useful for teaching the truth, rebuking error, correcting faults, and giving instructions for right living, so that the person who serves God may be fully qualified and equipped to do every kind of good deed' (2 Timothy 3:16–17).

> Does that mean God made people say what he wanted?

own personalities, spoke of their own special interests, and used their own gifts. That is why there is such variety in the Bible. It is a thoroughly human book.

But through all the human variety comes the voice of the living God – speaking to people then, and through them, speaking to us now.

God did not just put words into people's mouths. The Bible's writers were ordinary people of their times who spoke and wrote out of their own experience. They used their own language, and were concerned about things that were going on around them. They spoke about historical events, political decisions, social issues, religious affairs, personal joys and problems.

They expressed their

GOD STILL SPEAKS!

It may be very interesting to see how God has spoken to people in the past, but surely that's just the problem – it was all in the past! The Bible is a very ancient book. What has it got to do with us here and now?

Christians believe that the Bible is relevant today, because of three things about God:

● **God is living.** The God of the Bible is not confined to the Bible. He was there from before the beginning of the universe itself, and he did not quietly pass away as the last page of the Bible was written. He is still alive, and he still wants to communicate with people. He continues to speak to us using the Bible.

● **God is true.** Everything God does is true to himself. He is consistent. We can rely on him. He is not fickle and changeable.

In the same way, everything God says is true. We can trust God not to tell lies or mislead us with false information. On the contrary he himself is the origin and standard of all truth. So when the Bible writers said that God was speaking through them, they believed that what they spoke and wrote was true.

The Bible is true because God is true – so it is completely trustworthy. If we use it properly and carefully, it will not mislead us. Instead, it will show us the truth about God, the world, ourselves – and the truth about how we should live.

● **God is king.** The God who made us has authority over us. Like a king (but far more than any human king), he has the right to command us and to expect our obedience.

When God spoke to people in the time when the Bible was written, he spoke with authority. And the Bible still carries the authority of God. In it God speaks to us as our maker and king. He claims our attention and demands a response.

So when we open the Bible and begin to read it, we are exposing ourselves to the voice of the God who made us and who speaks to us with authority. It could change our lives! In fact, it is meant to.

USING THE BIBLE

On/off A radio won't say anything to you unless the power is switched on and you have tuned in. Neither will the Bible. We need to ask God to help us switch on to what he is saying.

Tone If you listen with the tone turned up, you miss the depth of the music. We can miss the depth of what the Bible has to say by only reading the parts we think are easy. We only get the depth and richness of it all when we explore the whole Bible.

Stereo speakers Two speakers are better than one. They give a fuller sound. The Bible also has two speakers: the Old and New Testaments. By listening to both we get God's complete message to us.

Aerial Without an aerial, a radio's reception is weak and distorted. To hear God speaking through the Bible, we need to be in touch with him in the first place.

Tuning in A radio allows you to tune in to a large number of different programmes. There is enormous variety in the Bible, too. This book is a guide to the frequencies available in the Bible. So keep your Bible handy as you read.

GETTING THE MESSAGE

The message of the Bible comes from God, but as we have also seen, it comes through people. The words of the Bible were first addressed to men and women in a wide variety of times and places, in a variety of ways, and for many different purposes. So if we are to get the message for ourselves, we need to understand some of this human variety.

We need to ask ourselves questions about the passage we are reading. In that way we will discover what it meant to those who first heard or read it. Only when we have grasped that original meaning can we go on to ask what it is saying to us now.

So why is it important to approach the Bible in this way?

● God doesn't change. By seeing how God spoke and acted in the past, we get a fuller picture of what he is like. This will help us to know what God is saying to us today – which is the whole point of reading the Bible. Our greatest desire as Christians is not just to know the Bible, but to know God.

● The message of the Bible. If we take seriously the original meaning of a passage, it will stop us twisting it to suit ourselves. Some cynical people say that you can make the Bible mean anything you like, and some people do. We cannot be so free and easy with it once we begin to understand what it meant originally.

So here are a few of the questions we need to ask in order to get the

message out of any Bible passage.

What is the background to this passage?

How does the **difference** between the background of this passage and my own situation affect the way I apply it? Are there **similarities** between then and now which can help me see the relevance of the passage to today?

Who was the author of this passage?

This will lead us to ask other questions. What was the writer's interest and purpose in writing this? Was he writing it for a particular person or people? Why did he put it like this? If he were alive now, what would I like to ask him? And (more importantly!), what might he want to say to me?

What kind of writing is this?

The Bible is not really a single book, but a library of books. The word Bible actually comes from a Greek word that means library. And in that library are all kinds of different writing.

So the questions we need to ask are . . .

● Is it plain narrative, which fills in the facts behind my faith?

● Is it teaching, which I should be learning?

● Is it commanding or challenging, calling for obedience?

● Is it prophetic or promising, calling for faith?

● Is it poetic or worshipful, calling for an emotional response?

● If the writer is using symbolic or pictorial language, is there a plain and obvious meaning behind his words?

Let's try out these three questions on a familiar Bible story – the parable of the Good Samaritan. We will see if they help us to discover a deeper meaning than we may have found before. The story is in Luke 10:25-37.

● What is the background to this passage? Jesus was talking to a teacher of the Jewish Law. This teacher knew that he should love his neighbour, but he wanted to know who qualified to be his neighbour.

In the story Jesus told, the priest and Levite were respected people – good and upright clergymen. A Samaritan, on the other hand, was deeply hated and despised for all sorts of reasons – historical, racial, social and religious.

The idea of a good Samaritan was unthinkable. Against the background of his own day, this story of Jesus was no homely tale. Instead, it was quite startling – a Tale of the Unexpected.

● Who was the author of this passage? Luke records this incident. And although the first three Gospels have so much material in common, this particular story is found only in Luke.

Luke is specially

interested in the way Jesus turns things upside down by his preaching of the Kingdom of God. His Gospel is full of the unexpected. Take a look at some other examples: Luke 1:52-53; 4:18-19; 10:13-15; 12:15-20; 18:9-14; 22:24-27.

So this story is an example of Luke's desire to show how Jesus challenges our prejudices.

● What kind of writing is this? The story comes within a Gospel, which means good news about Jesus Christ and what God has done through him. So we need to put ourselves in the shoes of the man Jesus was talking to. We can listen to the story as if Jesus were present and then respond to him through it.

The story itself is a parable. Parables were a device Jesus used to make people think and question. They were not just cosy, comfortable stories. Often they were deliberately shocking, as this one was.

We need to try to listen to it with the ears of those who first heard it. Then we should ask who, in our society, might fit the categories of priest, Levite and despised Samaritan.

The result will be a challenge to our prejudices and a fresh understanding of what it means to be a neighbour.

PICTURES OF THE BIBLE AT WORK

We began by comparing the Bible to a radio, as a means of communication. But of course, that is a picture unknown in the Bible itself! But there are various pictures the Bible uses to describe itself. Some of them will help us see how the Bible is meant to be used. They will help us to appreciate how we can get the most out of it practically.

A LAMP

'Your word is a lamp to guide me and a light for my path' (Psalm 119:105).

The Bible, God's word, gives light for the road we walk on. It gives us guidance for daily living. The writer of Psalm 119 was talking about a little oil lamp – not a floodlamp or magnesium flare. His lamp was one that would show you enough of the way ahead on a dark night for you to take the next few steps safely. That is usually the way God guides us – step by step.

MILK

'Be like new-born babies, always thirsty for the pure spiritual milk, so that by drinking it you may grow up' (1 Peter 2:2).

The spiritual milk Peter was talking about is the Bible. He pinpoints the main thing about milk – it is food for growth. Milk is the first and most important food for every child. It is balanced. It enables healthy growth for the bones and muscles. In the same way, the Bible is balanced food for the muscles of our faith. It helps us grow spiritually strong and mature.

We should not stay like babies in our faith and knowledge, but we should always have a baby's appetite – always thirsty, never satisfied for long, always coming back for more!

A SWORD

'Take the word of God as the sword which the Spirit gives you' (Ephesians 6:17).

A sword was meant to be kept sharp. The Bible can be like that when we allow it to get close to what we are really like inside. So we need to read it honestly. We should be prepared to face up to what it may show up in us – things we may not like to admit, and even things we have not been aware of before. Then we can bring those things frankly to God for him to put them right.

A sword, too, was a weapon to be used in battle. As Christians, we are involved in a battle against evil in the world and temptation and sin in our own lives. The Bible is a very effective weapon to use in that struggle.

So we need to read the Bible with faith, believing that God really means what he says, and that he keeps the promises he has put into it. Many people also find it helpful in everyday life to memorize Bible verses, so that they are always ready to face problems and temptation.

A SEED

'The seed is the word of God' (Luke 8:11).

Jesus said these words as he explained his famous parable of the sower. Now the great thing about seed is that it contains life. It has great potential. Seed in itself is not very exciting stuff to look at (just as many people mistakenly think the Bible is a bit dull), but its secret lies in what it can do. Once it is planted, it germinates, it grows, and eventually it bears fruit – reproducing and multiplying its own life.

The Bible, like seed, is God's living word. When it gets into a person's mind and heart, it brings new life. It bears fruit in practical ways – new desires, new habits, a new character. The Bible changes people! Or rather, God changes people through the living seed of his word.

GETTING THE BEST OUT OF YOUR BIBLE

Read it regularly. Like food and exercise, a 'little and often' is the best approach. If it is possible to set aside a short time each day for reading a passage from the Bible you will find it very helpful.

Do read it in a form you can understand. Use an up-to-date version that makes the meaning clear, such as the Good News Bible or the New International Version.

Read it systematically. If you just plunge into the Bible and start reading whatever you happen to see, you will soon get confused. The Bible readings given in this manual will help you to get more from the Bible.

Read it as a whole. That does not mean read it all at once! It means try to keep a balanced diet, as you do with food. Read in both Testaments. Read different kinds of writing. Try to see how one part sheds light on the meaning of other parts. See how certain themes come up in different ways in many places. Don't interpret one passage in such a way that it contradicts others. Instead, look for the meaning common to both, for it is all God's word.

Read it imaginatively. Go in for 'active' reading. Try to visualize the original situation, as if you were a news reporter. Put yourself into the mind and emotions of the writer, the characters, or those who first read it. Ask questions about what you are reading, and let it question and challenge you at the same time.

   Many people find it helpful to have a notebook to jot down their thoughts as they read a passage. This helps them to remember what they learn.

Respond to what you read. As we read the Bible, we can thank God for the privilege of hearing him speak to us. But that is also a great responsibility. Once we have heard God's word, then we are faced with the decision to obey and apply it honestly in our lives. The real test of our sincerity is not just how much we have read, but how much we have obeyed.

Don't try to read it all from cover to cover right away. Remember that the Bible is a library of books – you would not try to read all the books in a library straight away! Read selectively. You might follow the system of readings in this manual first, and then read certain books at a time.

Don't worry if you cannot understand a passage immediately. Understand and enjoy the parts that are clear. The Bible is like a great ocean. It has a sandy beach with shallows where even children can safely play. It has deeper parts where adults can swim. But it also has vast depths that we may never get to the bottom of.

Don't look for complicated and obscure meanings. Look for the plain meaning by reading it clearly as it is. And if a particular passage does seem to have a lot of symbolism in it, don't be dazzled and fascinated by clever people and their fanciful theories.

Don't use the Bible like a lucky dip or a horoscope, by just opening it at random and expecting some magic word. It is the living word of the living God, and we must read it seriously and carefully.

Don't limit yourself to a diet of 'golden promises' or 'blessed thoughts'. That way you can't lose! Of course the Bible is full of many great promises which give us strength, hope, or comfort. But God has many other things to say to us through the Bible. There are words of warning, rebuke or challenge – which we must not miss.

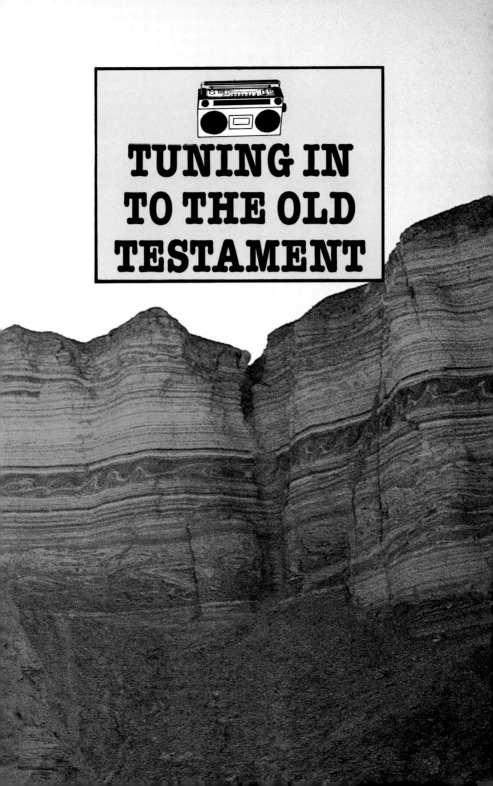

TUNING IN TO THE OLD TESTAMENT

Do you have a hope that human history is leading somewhere, that sometime it will make sense, and that there will be a better future? The Old Testament not only shares your hope, it shows you how it will come true.

Do you have an active social conscience? Are you concerned for the agonizing political, economic and social issues which surround us, wanting to see justice and peace in the world? You won't find a keener vision or a stronger ally than the Old Testament.

Are you warmed by the great spiritual tradition of the church, with its worship, rituals, songs and prayers? You may be surprised to discover how much of it is directly taken from the robust worship of Israel in the Old Testament.

Are you fascinated by humanity itself, with our enormous potential for goodness and creativity, yet with all the horrific mess we have got into? The Old Testament explains both sides of human nature.

Are you interested in what Christianity teaches about God, about creation and the world we live in? Come and find out in the Old Testament.

Are you sometimes overwhelmed by the suffering in the world – especially the suffering of innocent people – or the apparent futility of so much of life for so many people? You will find people like yourself wrestling with these problems in the Old Testament.

1

THE BIBLE'S FIRST HALF

As everyone knows, the centre of the Christian faith is Jesus Christ himself. And the Bible is the text-book of Christianity. Yet when we come to the Bible for the first time, we discover that Jesus doesn't arrive on the scene until well into the second half of the book, when we reach the New Testament.

The first part (and by far the larger part) of the Christian Bible is called the Old Testament. The Old Testament contains the writings that the Jewish people held sacred for many centuries before the birth of Jesus Christ. Why are all these writings still kept part of the Christian Bible? The simple answer is that Jesus was a Jew. As a result, he knew the Old Testament very well.

Like any Jewish boy, Jesus was brought up to know very thoroughly the Jewish scriptures. He used and quoted the scriptures often in his teaching. He also saw himself and all that he had come to do in the light of the Old Testament.

So if we are interested to know about Jesus and how he saw himself, then we need to know something of the Old Testament.

What is in the Old Testament? As we read it, we should expect to find the origins of the great and exciting features that we associate with Christianity. If the Christian faith is a building, then the New Testament is the upper storey and roof. But the foundation, the lower storeys and the whole shape of the building is provided by the Old Testament.

For all these reasons and many more, come and tune in to the Old Testament and listen to what God has to say to us through it.

THE VOICES OF THE OLD TESTAMENT

If the Bible is like a radio, then as we begin to use it we may at first find it all rather confusing – like listening to all the radio stations at random.

It is only when we get familiar with the different voices on the radio that we can understand what is going on.

We can tell the voice of the newsreader, and the different tone of a sports commentator. Then there is the disc-jockey, the economic correspondent or the quiz-master.

We understand and react according to the different voices we hear.

Now we have to do something similar to get in on the Old Testament wavelength. It has a great variety of voices – many different kinds of literature. We need to sort out who is talking as well as what is being said. Here are some of the voices we hear most as we read the Old Testament.

Storyteller

Everyone loves a good story, and the art of story-telling was a much respected feature of ancient societies. In Israel's case, the narratives which tell the story take up almost half of the Old Testament. The importance of these historical narratives is that they ground our faith in facts.

The religions of Judaism and Christianity did not come into being by men sitting down, talking and imagining what God might be like. Both faiths claim instead that God himself has taken the initiative. They point to certain events which have happened in history and claim that God was active in them. He did this to show us what he is like.

There are two important things we should remember when listening to the voice of storytellers.
● **It is about God.** The Old Testament stories are not primarily about men and women. God is the central figure. Either he is visibly active on stage, or you can see him at work behind the scenes.
● **It is a matter of fact.** Because the narrators take God as a matter of fact, there is no embarrassment about recording him in direct action. Some of the stories include the supernatural or miraculous. They are there not just to excite us, but to point to God himself.

There are also stories that lack the miraculous, but where God is clearly at work in ordinary human affairs. This is true of the Joseph stories in Genesis and the narratives of Saul, Samuel, David and Solomon.

Commander

A great deal of the Old Testament seems to be giving orders! Whole sections, especially in the early books, have a very authoritative tone of voice.

What is it all for?
● **It shows us God's authority.**
A person can only give orders to others if he has been put in charge and has authority. The commands and laws in the Old Testament show that God has the right to demand our obedience. He is in charge. In the Old and New Testaments morality isn't a question of 'what I like', or even 'what the majority of people like', but 'what God commands'.

That's why listening to the voice of the Bible is not always comfortable. Sometimes it shakes and shocks us.
● **It shows us God's love.** Sometimes people think that law is the opposite of love. But it isn't. Parents tell their children what to do and what not to do because they love them and want to guide them. The fact that God gives us commands shows that our behaviour really matters to him. He doesn't sit up in heaven with a shrug and say, 'Oh, please youselves then, see if I care!' The real point behind the Law is to help us respond to what he has done for us.
● **It shows us ourselves.** The law of the Old Testament is like a mirror. In it, we see how far short we fall of God's standards. In this way it prepares us for the good news of the New Testament. We can see that we need to be forgiven and saved by Jesus because we have not loved God or our neighbour as the Law commands.

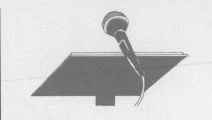

Expert

The Old Testament is also full of advice given by experts:

● **The priests.** The job of the priests was partly to teach and guide the people. They were a kind of community advice service.

Among the things they taught was the meaning of the various laws, rituals and festivals. Some of these parts of the Old Testament, such as Leviticus, are like a visual aid to show us truths about God's holiness and our need of forgiveness.

Later on in the history of Israel, when the people disobeyed the Law of God, the prophets blamed the priests for failing to teach the Law entrusted to them.

● **The wise men.** There was another kind of expert – the sages, or wise men. This was an international phenomenon, for there were also famous schools of wisdom in ancient Egypt and Babylon. In Israel the voice of wisdom flourished especially during the reign of Solomon, who had wide international contacts.

The books of the Bible that belong to this wisdom literature are Job, Proverbs, Ecclesiastes and the Song of Solomon.

Job is a dramatic wrestling with the problem of innocent suffering.

Proverbs deals with a vast array of everyday life: personal relationships, work and leisure, wisdom and folly, social care and generosity.

Ecclesiastes is brutally honest about how futile life can seem.

The Song of Solomon cheers us up again with the beauty and joy of human love.

Preacher

The books of the prophets are all collected together at the end of the Old Testament. They are divided into major ones (the three long books of Isaiah, Jeremiah and Ezekiel) and the minor ones (all the shorter books). Although placed together in the Bible, they did not all do their work at the same time.

The prophets were God's high explosive! They were sent to shake people out of their complacency, false security, or outright wickedness. They came with a blunt claim to be speaking the very words of God. What they had to say was often uncomfortable – and some of them had a very uncomfortable time themselves at the hands of their hearers.

It can be easy to think of a prophet as someone who merely predicts the future. But although many of the Old Testament prophecies do include visions of the future, they had a much more important job. They were sent with a piece of God's mind on current affairs of their own time.

So unless we match together a particular piece of prophetic writing with the historical affairs of that time, it will probably not make much sense. To open a prophetic book at random and start reading is like turning on the radio to a heated and serious discussion programme where you haven't a clue what they are talking about.

But when we do discover the real-life situation behind the prophecy, we can often see how similar it is to some issue or problem today.

The Mystery Voice

All the prophets make some use of picture language to express what God was doing, or was going to do. But in the Bible a way of writing developed which depended entirely on symbolic and visionary language. This is called apocalyptic literature.

The word 'apocalyptic' means to 'uncover' what is hidden. This kind of writing was regarded as a peep behind the scenes into the mystery of God's ways with the world, in the present and the future.

Apocalyptic became more popular in Jewish literature between the Old and New Testaments. But in the Old Testament it is found in Daniel 7–12, Isaiah 24–27 and Zechariah 1–8, where there is highly pictorial imagery.

This kind of voice is often difficult to make out clearly, and it is easy to fall into weird and wonderful interpretations of it. However we can understand it better when we see the difference between prophecy and apocalyptic.

● **Prophecy is usually intended as a warning.** It says, 'This is what will happen, unless you change. But if you do change your ways, then this is what will happen. . .'

● **Apocalyptic is usually intended as an encouragement.** It says, 'This is what is really going on behind all the outward appearances of world power-politics. God is still in control and these are the events he has decreed will happen. So be prepared and endure them faithfully. In the end, the wicked will be destroyed and God will deliver his own people.'

Worshipper

The Bible is not a one-way conversation. It is the record of a relationship between God and his people Israel. So what they had to say to him is also included. The Book of Psalms is right at the heart of the Bible. It is the very human response of Israel to God – sometimes in joy and praise, but often in suffering and despair. It is worship from real life.

The Psalms and other prayers and praises in the Old Testament are poetry. But they are not there just for our literary appreciation. They were meant to be sung and danced to. So the worshipping voice not only speaks to us, it also calls us to join in and share its living flow of faith, praise and prayer. For the God it worships is our God too.

📖 PASSAGES

☐ Old Testament Voices

Storyteller
1 Samuel 3:1–21
Commander
Exodus 20:1–17
Expert
Proverbs 3:1–18
Preacher
Isaiah 1:1–20
Mystery voice
Daniel 7:1–28
Worshipper
Psalm 8
Worshipper
Psalm 103

IN THE BEGINNING

Genesis. . . genetics . . . genes are words that all have to do with the beginning and shaping of life. The Book of Genesis not only begins the Bible story, it also programmes it.

It lays the foundation and gives the outline plan of the whole structure. Most of the big themes that are part of the structure of the Christian faith follow the shape laid down by Genesis. The windows, doors and decorations come later, but Genesis determines the basic shape.

GOD THE CREATOR

The Bible begins with a majestic description of everything that exists – and asserts that God created the lot. Nothing existed before he made it, and nothing exists that he did not make. This is God's world, for he made it.

The opening chapters of Genesis tell us a number of things about God, the world and ourselves.
● **God is supreme.** The account of creation begins with the words, 'In the beginning God. . .'. It paints a picture of God who only has to say the word, and it is done. God is the source of everything that exists, and so everything is under his control.
● **The earth is good.** God made the earth, and he created everything that was necessary for life. But he did more than that. By filling the earth with colours, strange creatures and spectacular sights and sounds, he showed that he cares about the variety and richness of life. All that God made was good.
● **Mankind is special.** God did not make people as just another ingredient in his creation. Men and women were made in 'God's image', reflecting something of

his character. They enjoyed a close relationship with him, and were also given special responsibilities. They were to look after the earth on God's behalf, and to use its resources with skill and wisdom.

❝Then God said, 'And now we will make human beings; they will be like us and resemble us. They will have power over the fish, the birds, and all animals, domestic and wild, large and small.' So God created human beings, making them to be like himself . . . God looked at everything he had made, and he was very pleased. ❞
Genesis 1:26–27, 31

The creation account centres on the idea that each seventh day is a day of rest from work. On this day, people are free to relax and to worship God for his love and power.

The natural world has always fascinated explorers and adventurers. The Bible tells us that God was pleased with the world he had created.

THE FALL

The story of Adam and Eve in Genesis 2 and 3 is well known to many people. Many cartoons and jokes have been based on the story. But the subject it is dealing with is very unfunny indeed. It tells us how mankind has ended up in the horrific mess the world is in.

The story is quickly sketched in. God creates the natural world, and then makes man and woman to live in his world and run it on his behalf. However, Adam and Eve give in to the temptation to disobey God. They end up cut off from their earlier intimacy with God. They blame God and each other and live in a world that is cursed because of their sin.

The whole catastrophic event is called the fall.

Sin

The fact that all men are sinful is another basic Bible truth taught in Genesis. Here are three things about sin that Genesis teaches us before we even get past its first eleven chapters.

● **Entry.** The entry of sin had little to do with sex or an apple as cartoons make believe. It began with doubt: doubt about God's goodness and honesty. Then it became a rebellion: a thought-out, reasoned act of rebellion. Then it became disobedience: an outward act. Then it was shared: Adam and Eve became partners in evil. So sin took root in every part of mankind – spiritual, mental, physical and social.

● **Extent.** Every part of the human personality was affected and polluted by sin. 'The Lord saw how wicked everyone on earth was and how evil their thoughts were all the time . . .' (Genesis 6:5).

● **Effect.** Sin destroyed all the relationships God had made. It destroyed the harmony between people and God. Adam and Eve hid from him after their sin.

It destroyed the harmony between person and person – with injustice, oppression and the horrible fruits of selfishness and pride.

It put people at odds with the physical environment. Adam was told that the cursed earth would resist and frustrate his efforts.

Sin is serious. The Bible tells us this, and we know it is true from our own experience. Once we begin to grasp how serious sin is, we can appreciate more vividly the Bible's story of God's conquest of sin. This conquest reached its climax in the Easter events of Jesus Christ.

The spread of sin

Once sin had entered human life it made its presence felt in ever-widening circles. The story of Cain and Abel (Genesis 4) is a graphic study of jealousy, anger, violence and murder. It also shows that God still held people accountable for one another. 'Where is your brother?' he asked Cain.

Eventually the wickedness of humanity became unbearable and brought on the judgement of the flood. But God rescued a man called Noah and his family. In this way God combined judgement and salvation in the same act, something that happens throughout the Bible.

The growth of nations after the flood is described in Genesis 10. This is clearly a very ancient account of different races and civilizations at some point in human history. It shows us that God's actions in judgement and salvation took place in the real world of geographical nations and international politics – not in some mythical world.

That real human world was in danger

A main theme of the Bible is that men and women have rebelled against God. Human evil has affected everything in our world.

Is creation really true?

Many books have been written about the problem of relating the creation stories to what scientists tell us about the beginnings of life on earth.

Some people insist that every detail of Genesis has to be taken literally. Others say that Genesis gives us no solid facts about the origins of life. Here are a few pointers to help us think through the problem.

● **How and why.** The creation stories were never intended to be scientific descriptions of how it all happened. Their main aim is to tell us that it is God's work.

Science has always tried to answer the 'How. . .?' questions. In recent centuries it has done so with increasing detail and success. But even if it could explain how the universe works, we would still have questions. 'Why is it there?' 'Did someone design it?' 'Why are we here?'

These are the really important questions – and they cannot be answered by scientific enquiry. But they are the questions the Bible is concerned with. If God had written the account of the creation of the world in the technical language of all the sciences, nobody could have understood it for thousands of years, and even today most of us would not understand it.

● **Different descriptions.** There need be no contradiction between the Bible's teaching about creation and scientific theory and description. They are different kinds of account of the same thing.

Suppose you are a builder and you build a house for a friend. You will need all kinds of technical drawings, building regulations and planning permission.

After your friend has moved in, he writes to you with a simple account of what for him is his home. He tells you how he has decorated it, and what the garden is like. And he thanks you for such a well-designed and carefully-built house.

It would be silly to say that the technical documents contradicted the personal letter. They are both true. One is an accurate explanation of the house as an object. The other is an appreciative description of the house as a home. The first explains how it was built. The second explains why.

It is just as silly for people to say that science contradicts or disproves the Bible. Or to say that if you believe the Bible you must reject science. Their purpose and method are different.

● **Room for manoeuvre.** It is possible to hold different views on the details of the story without denying that it is God's word, inspired by him. But it is quite wrong to say that my view is the only interpretation that is true, and if you don't accept my interpretation you don't believe the Bible. We need to avoid attitudes like this.

of over-reaching itself in its arrogance. The story of the tower of Babel typifies human pride.

So the early chapters of Genesis close with mankind in a state of international confusion. Scattered and divided by sin, people appear to be far from God. What can God do now? Is there any hope for mankind? The answer to these questions begins in Genesis 12.

THE FATHERS OF ISRAEL

At Genesis 12 we step into two kinds of history at the same time. There is human history that can be given dates. But Genesis 12 also signals the start of the history of Israel's faith in God, with Abraham, their ancestor, or father.

● **The fathers in human history.**
During this century archaeology has shed light on the ancient civilizations of the Middle East. The stories of Israel's fathers (Abraham, Isaac and Jacob) fit

What is a covenant?

A covenant is a promise between two parties which is made into a formal and binding commitment, usually by some ceremony. In the ancient world these ceremonies often included an animal sacrifice and a shared covenant meal.

A good example of a covenant today is marriage. There, two people make promises to each other in a ceremony, and their contract is bound by the law.

There are a number of different covenants in the Bible:
● **God made a covenant with Noah,** for the benefit of the world (Genesis 8:20—9:17).
● **He made a covenant with Abraham** (Genesis 15).
● **He made a covenant with Israel** at Mount Sinai (Exodus 19:3–6, and 24:3–11).
● **A later covenant was made with King David** (2 Samuel 7:8–16).

But it was Jesus who made the new and final covenant (Luke 22:19–20). The sacrifice was his own death. The covenant meal was the Last Supper. The promises God made are open to all people.

authentically into the culture of that time. Their travel and migration fit in with that era of political confusion.

Many details found on inscriptions, law codes and legal documents from that time agree with the descriptions of life in Genesis. Details that ring true include personal names, place names, household customs, terms of employment, the way that land was purchased.

Again, the Bible is concerned with real people. It tells us about the politics, geography and culture of the time.

● **The fathers and the faith of Israel.**
The Israelites called Abraham, Isaac and Jacob 'the fathers'. This was not only because of their physical link as a family. The promises God had made to these men were the foundation of the nation.

God called Abram (his name before God changed it to Abraham) to leave his own country and go to Canaan. He made him a promise with three specific parts.

To give him descendants who would be a great nation.
To give that nation the land of Canaan.
To use his descendants to bless all the nations.

The Lord said to Abram,

❝Leave your native land, your relatives, and your father's home, and go to a country that I am going to show you. I will give you many descendants and they will become a great nation. I will bless you and make your name famous, so that you will be a blessing. I will bless those who bless you, but I will curse those who curse you. And through you I will bless all the nations. Genesis 12:1–3 ❞

This promise was sealed as a covenant. The rest of the Old Testament shows how God kept his side of the covenant with Abraham. The people of Israel knew that they owed their survival as a nation to God's faithfulness, rather than to their military strength.

Genesis 12 explains how the Jews came to believe they were God's chosen people. It also shows why they believed this. It was not so that they could feel superior and privileged. Instead, they were told that through them God's salvation would go to all the nations.

The Bible tells us that this part of the covenant was only fulfilled by Jesus Christ, descendant of Abraham.

📖 PASSAGES TO READ

LAND OF HOPE AND GLORY

One of the great arts of storytelling is to keep the reader or listener in suspense. The narrators of the Bible are expert at it.

Take Abraham. God tells him at seventy-five years of age that he will have a host of descendants – and he hadn't even one son yet! Here he is again at ninety-nine and still no son! Has God forgotten? The story of Joseph is also shot through with suspense and surprise.

Genesis ends on a happy note with the descendants of Abraham comfortably settled in Egypt as guests of Pharaoh, the ruler. But no sooner do we open the book of Exodus than we are landed in suspense again. Centuries have passed. Less hospitable pharaohs are in power. The guests have become slaves. Far from enjoying a land of their own, the descendants of Abraham are held captive and oppressed in a foreign land.

What can God do now? Stay tuned!

The full story can be read in the books of Exodus to Joshua. These books also include large sections of laws and instructions. The main narrative appears in Exodus 1–19; 24; 32–34; Numbers 10–25; Deuteronomy 1–3; 31–34; Joshua 1–12.

THE EXODUS

What happened to Israel at the time of their great escape from Egypt became their national epic. It was as important to Israel (and still is to Jews) as the cross and resurrection of Jesus are to Christians.

One writer of the Bible said:

❝Search the past, the time before you were born, all the way back to the time when God created man on the earth. Search the entire earth.

Has anything as great as this ever happened before? Has anyone ever heard of anything like this? Have any people ever lived after hearing a god speak to them from a fire, as you have? Has any god ever dared to go and take a people from another nation and make them his own, as the Lord your God did for you in Egypt?

Before your very eyes he used his great power and strength; he brought plagues and war, worked miracles and wonders, and caused terrifying things to happen. The Lord has shown you this, to prove to you that he alone is God and there is no other. ❞

Deuteronomy 4:32–35

● **The exodus involved a new revelation of God's name.** A young man, Moses, was called by God to go down to Egypt to liberate his people. When this happened, Moses wanted to know the name of the God who would do this. God said he was the God of Abraham, Isaac and Jacob. But he also announced a new name: Yahweh. He explained its meaning as 'I am who I am'.

The rest of the story shows why God used this name. It was to remind his people that he was faithful and consistent. He had remembered his promise to Abraham and he would keep it. His people would know who he was and what he was like when they saw what he could do.

So Yahweh is the great personal name of God in the Old Testament. It is always associated with his power to deliver and with his promises to his people, as proved in the exodus.

The name Yahweh appears in English Bibles as 'Jehovah', or 'the Lord'.

● **The exodus was like an act of purchase.** The Israelites used the word 'redeem' to describe what God had done for them. 'Redemption' was originally a commercial act of buying back property that had been lost or mortgaged, or people who had been enslaved by debt or war.

In the exodus, God had bought back Israel for himself. From then on they were to belong wholly to him, throughout every succeeding generation. He had delivered them from slavery and death. Now they would be his special people. That was something to be glad about and take great comfort from.

Isaiah the prophet, speaking on God's behalf, expressed it like this:

At the beginning of the Bible, the Israelites were a bedraggled group of refugees on the run from the country that had enslaved them. It was to these people that God spoke, rather than to the strong and powerful.

❝Fear not, for I have redeemed you; I have called you by name; you are mine. Isaiah 43:1 ❞

● **The exodus was to be remembered by the Israelites in their treatment of one another.** It is no accident that the first law given to Israel after the Ten Commandments is about the treatment of slaves. The memory of their own slavery was fresh. God had been merciful to them. They should be generous to others.

● **The exodus became a model for God's future actions.** Whenever Israel again suffered defeat or oppression, they looked to God to act in the same way. This happened especially when they were taken into exile in Babylon centuries later.

In the New Testament, we are told that God sent Jesus to be the Redeemer of the world. The early Jewish Christians saw it as a wonderful new exodus for those enslaved by sin. As in the Old Testament, those who have been redeemed by God through Jesus become his special, purchased people.

That affects how we live too.

SINAI

Three months after leaving Egypt, months of hardship and grumbling, the rabble of Hebrew refugee slaves arrived at Mount Sinai. There God began to mould them into a nation.

The training began with a terrifying audio-visual aid. As God came down to Mount Sinai, there was an earthquake, thunderstorm, fire, cloud and noise. The events described in Exodus 19 made a deep and lasting impression on Israel's national memory. Their God was a God of unapproachable holiness, not to be trifled with.

At Sinai, God made his covenant with Israel as a nation, through Moses as his go-between. This covenant, which included the giving of the Ten Commandments and other laws, is sometimes called the Sinai covenant, to distinguish it from the covenant with Abraham.

The account of the covenant-making ceremony is in Exodus 24. Israel learnt some very important things about God and themselves during their stay at Sinai:

● **He was the only God.** Most nations at the time believed in gods who were confined to the boundaries of the nation. They were expected to provide crops, good weather, prosperity, and social stability.

But here was a God who intervened in historical and political events with amazing power. Not only that, but he was unrestricted by any locality. He was as powerful in the desert as in Egypt, and would prove the same in Canaan.

No wonder the Canaanites were scared stiff when they heard the reports about the God of Israel! No wonder the Israelites came to believe that he was not just a unique god, but the only living God of all the earth.

Deuteronomy puts it like this:

❝The Lord alone led his people without the help of a foreign god. 'I and I alone, am God; no other god is real.'** Deuteronomy 32:12, 39 ❞

This was the beginning of the central feature of the Jewish faith. They believed in monotheism – that there is only one, true, living God.

● **The covenant was started by God.** If the relationship between God and Israel could be compared to a marriage (as some prophets later did), it was God who did the proposing! And he led up to his proposal by giving proof of his love in delivering Israel from Egypt.

The order of the Bible story is very important here, as it usually is. God did not send Moses down into Egypt with the two tables of the Ten Commandments tucked under his cloak, to say to the Hebrew slaves, 'Here you are. This is God's Law. If you can manage to keep it for a few centuries, God will reward you by rescuing you from this cruel oppression.'

No. God acted first. He took the initiative. He came down to Egypt 'with a mighty hand and outstretched arm' and swept his people to freedom. He did so out of love and faithfulness to his earlier promise to Abraham.

Only then did he say to them, 'Now that I have rescued you, this is how I want you to live. I have freed you to be my people. I ask you to keep my Law, out of gratitude to me as your God'.

Moses told the people of Israel what God said:

❝ You saw what I, the Lord, did to the Egyptians and how I carried you as an eagle carries her young on her wings, and brought you here to me.

Now, if you will obey me and keep my covenant, you will be my own people. The whole earth is mine, but you will be my chosen people, a people dedicated to me alone, and you will serve me as priests. ❞

Exodus 19:4–6

● **The covenant was kept alive by God.** No sooner had the covenant been ratified than the people broke it! Moses had gone up the mountain to receive instructions from God. The people became fed up waiting for him and pressurized Aaron, Moses' right-hand man, into making an idol for them.

Moses returned from the mountain and found them worshipping a golden calf. In great anger, he broke the two stone tablets of the Law, symbolizing the broken covenant.

However, when God said he was going to destroy the people, Moses turned to prayer. He pleaded for the people to be forgiven, reminding God of his promise to Abraham and of the covenant promises made at Sinai.

The story of all this can be read in Exodus 32–34, and it goes on to show how God amazingly forgave and pardoned the people, and remade the covenant with them. Right from the very start, Israel knew that their covenant relationship with God was not only started by him, it was also kept alive by him.

WANDERING IN THE DESERT

The generation that left Egypt did not enter the promised land of Canaan. They left Sinai and arrived at the oasis of Kadesh Barnea. Moses sent out spies to reconnoitre the land, but they returned with a 10 to 2 verdict against trying to invade it.

The people's morale failed and that generation did not get another chance. Even Moses, their leader, was not to enter Canaan. They spent the next forty years wandering in the desert and died there.

The nation learned another vital lesson about God through the experience. He could provide for them and protect them. Food and water kept them alive, though they grumbled that the menu was better in Egypt! And their enemies were defeated in battle.

Eventually a new generation of Israel

The tent of God's presence

A lot of the book of Exodus is taken up with a detailed description of the tent of God's presence. This tent was at the centre of Israel's worship of God during their time in the desert.

In Exodus 25–31 God gives Moses the plans for the tent, and his instructions for the priests who would serve in it. Exodus 35–40 describe it being constructed. The details may seem very compli-cated, but in fact the tent and its contents were really quite basic and simple. They needed to be, as the whole lot had to be easy to put together, take apart, and carry around on their travels.

● There was an enclosed outer courtyard, with an altar for animal sacrifice and a bath for the priests to wash before entering the tent itself.

● The outer part of the tent housed an altar for burning incense, a table with loaves on, and a seven-branched candlestick.

● The inner room (called the holy of holies) contained the ark of the covenant with the Ten Commandments. It symbolized the very closest presence of God. Only the high priest could enter it, once a year, to represent the people before God, with the blood of a sacrifice for their sins.

This tent was important to Israel because it showed them that God was present among them. It was carried with them wherever they journeyed.

was camped in Moab – just the other side of Jordan from the land of promise.

THE CONQUEST

The Book of Joshua opens with words that the reader might have wondered if he was ever going to hear. At last God tells the people, under their new leader, Joshua, to get up, cross the River Jordan and invade the land he had promised to give them.

Joshua 1 is a great chapter for those who are wanting to serve God – especially if it means starting out on something new or facing the unknown, as Joshua did after the death of Moses.

● **There was God's command.** 'Get up and get on with the job I have set before you. Be strong and do it!' (Joshua 1:2,6)
● **There was God's condition.** 'Make sure you obey me and do things my way.' (Joshua 1:7,8)
● **There was God's company.** 'I will always be with you, just as I was with Moses.' (Joshua 1:5,9)

Joshua 2–12 relates the stirring events of the conquest of the land. It starts with the crossing of the River Jordan and the fall of Jericho. It continues with the rapid military campaigns in the centre, south and north of the country which destroyed the power bases of the local kings.

Archaeology confirms the destruction of many of these small fortified city-states at a time consistent with the arrival of the Israelites.

The initial conquest was followed by a very long period when Israel's grip on the land became slowly firmer. The original inhabitants, not surprisingly, resisted the Israelite invaders fiercely. Some territory (including Jerusalem itself) was not captured until the time of King David.

Was the conquest fair?

The Israelites invaded and took over a land that had not been their own. And in the process they exterminated many of the people who lived there. This raises moral question marks in many people's minds. Why did God command this to be done?

● **Israel believed this to be divine judgement on the Canaanites.** Centuries earlier, God told Abraham that he was postponing the take-over of the land 'until they became so wicked that they must be punished'. What is known of Canaanite religious and social practices shows that they did include some horrific things. They practised child-sacrifice, as well as sexual perversions and ritual prostitution. The New Testament also accepts the conquest as judgement on the Canaanites for their accumulated sins (see Hebrews 11:31).
● **The Israelites were punished when they did the same.** They too were invaded many times, and in the end they were ejected from the land for two generations. God showed consistency in his moral judgement. The conquest was not just a one-sided piece of favouritism.
● **The existence of Israel was at stake.** They needed a land to survive. Israel was

Bizarre religious practices still characterize some areas of the world today. The Israelites were told not to imitate the religions of the countries around them.

THE LAW

God gave his Law to Israel as part of his agreement with the nation.

Clearly, the Law is a very important part of the Old Testament. But it can be difficult to know where to find it and how to sort it out.

Where to find the Law

The first five books of the Old Testament (known as the books of Moses) make up the Law. But these books contain a lot of narrative as well. Most of the actual laws can be found in four fairly well defined legal blocks.

● **The Ten Commandments** (Exodus 20:1–17, Deuteronomy 5:6–22). This is the foundation block of Old Testament Law. It gives the basic requirements that God makes of his people.

The Ten Commandments are the fundamental boundary posts for the conduct of God's people.

● **The 'Book of the Covenant'** (Exodus 21–23). This is the name given to a whole code of laws. This code was used when God and Israel first made the covenant, described in Exodus 24.

There are instructions about justice and compassion for the poor. The laws concerning slaves are especially humane, no doubt because Israel had been rescued from slavery.

● **The Levitical Law** (Leviticus). This book is mainly taken up with regulations for the duties of the priests.

The most important chapter is Leviticus 19, which begins, 'Be holy, because I, the Lord your God, am holy.' Its laws are very down to earth.

● **The Deuteronomic Law** (Deuteronomy 12–26). Deuteronomy is the Law, as it was preached by Moses. Many old laws from the earlier codes are given fresh interpretations, or new reasons to motivate people to obey them.

There are also new laws concerned with humanity, generosity and kindness. All of it is repeatedly set in the context of what God has done for Israel. In return, their love and gratitude should make them want to obey him.

How to sort it out

Each block of law contains all kinds of material. There is material that is instantly recognizable as law – legal obligations or prohibitions, with punishments and compensations. But there is other material which is more like advice. And some instructions could never have been enforced in a lawcourt. Here are the broad categories of Israel's Law.

Criminal law
Concerned with offences against society.

God the highest authority in the state. So offences against God treated as serious crimes.

These offences punished by the death penalty, because they threatened to bring the wrath of God down on the whole nation.

Most criminal offences stem from the breaking of the Ten Commandments.

Exodus 21:12–17
Exodus 22:20
Deuteronomy 22:22

Civil law

Concerned with disputes between citizens, in which no major covenant violation is involved.

Begin with 'If. . .', or 'When. . .', go on to describe a situation or event, then lay down what is to be done.

Often some form of compensation paid to the wronged person.

> Exodus 21:18–25
> Exodus 22:5–15

Laws for worship

Concerned with sacrifices, rituals, offerings, tithes, dietary and hygiene rules, festivals and holy days.

Also included laws to do with agriculture, such as not farming the land each seventh year, providing for the poor during harvest and giving a tenth of the crop to the poor.

> Exodus 23:10–19
> Deuteronomy
> 14:22–29

Family law

Families and wider kinship groups had a very important place in society. This included a judicial role.

Head of household had legal authority over his dependants in many areas of life. Included marriage and divorce, taking and releasing slaves, discipline of children.

Because of the importance of the family, laws were designed to protect it and preserve its land and property.

> Leviticus 25:23–28,
>   35–55
> Deuteronomy
>   21:15–17
> Deuteronomy 25:5–10

Charitable laws

Concerned with protection of the weak, justice for the poor, impartiality, generosity, care for strangers and immigrants.

Not just based on human decency but on God's character: 'This is what God is like, and so this is what he asks of you.'

> Exodus 22:21–27;
>   23:4–9
> Leviticus 19:9–10,
>   14–18, 32–34
> Deuteronomy 22:1–4,
>   6–8; 23:15–16;
>   24:5–6, 10–22

Old Testament geometry

There are many different kinds of law in the first five books of the Old Testament. But behind all these different laws are some basic underlying principles.

The social triangle. Old Testament Law reflects the three angles of Old Testament society.

God stood at the head of Israel. He brought the nation into existence, initiated the covenant and gave them their Law. So the Law assumes that people are answerable to God for their behaviour.

The land was also important. It was a proof of Israel's relationship with God. The land was also a practical responsibility God had given Israel.

The family stood at the centre of this triangle of relationships. It was important spiritually, socially, and economically. The Law was concerned to protect and preserve family life in each of these three ways.

The life and property parallels. Parallel lines never meet. They do not intersect, and so have no common point. This is a good way of expressing the Old Testament's attitude to human life and material property. They are on different levels and are never allowed to be equated with each other, or measured out together.

Human life is sacred because God created

people in his own image. Material goods are ultimately owned by God and come from him as a gift and a trust. This is why the Old Testament Law places stronger emphasis on the rights of persons (including slaves) than on rights of property. No offence involving property was punishable by death.

But for the same reason, the compulsory death penalty for murder could not be reduced to the payment of a fine to the relatives of the murdered person. Life was not to be measured in terms of things.

People matter more than things. That is a principle that is at the heart of Old Testament law.

The all-inclusive circle. The sheer variety of laws in the Old Testament can be bewildering. But it shows up how the whole of life was included in their scope.

The Law ranged from the most intensely private sphere of personal hygiene to the public arena of international politics – and everything in between. There was no part of life where you could say, 'It doesn't matter what I do; God isn't interested in this'.

This principle of Old Testament Law is carried over into the New Testament too. Jesus is seen as Lord of all, and everything is to be done as for him.

The right-angle of love. We sometimes think that law and love are opposites. But this is not so in the Bible. According to Jesus, the ultimate basis of the Law in the Old Testament was love.

It is a love that works in two directions. Vertically, it is love for God. To love God is to obey him. Horizontally, it is love for other people. To love your neighbour is to put his best interests first – even if he is one who hates you, or is engaged in a legal dispute with you.

You cannot have a right-angle without two lines. And you cannot have Old Testament Law without both these directions. The prophets had to keep reminding Israel of this. People thought they could worship God and claim to love him, when they were busy exploiting one another.

God would have none of it. Neither would Jesus. This principle unites both Old and New Testaments.

God's chosen method of bringing salvation to the whole of mankind. So it was vital that the nation should have a secure home in which to live.

The land God gave

The land was one of the major themes in the faith of Old Testament Israel. And the most important thing about the land was that it was a gift. Israel had a land to live in because God, quite simply, had given it to them.

This had important effects on Israel's life and faith.
● **It kept Israel dependent.** They had no natural right to any land. The one they had they owed to God's grace. So they knew that they had no claim over him, as if he were just a figurehead for their nationalism or a territorial mascot. Rather the reverse. Without him there would have been no nation and no land.
● **It showed God was dependable.** He had kept his promise to Abraham. The promised land was now the possessed land. God's faithfulness to his promise

had overcome all obstacles: the Egyptians, the grumblings of the Israelites, the attacks of their enemies, the resistance of the Canaanites.

The land itself was solid proof of the character of God – he was utterly trustworthy and dependable. Every harvest reminded them of that.

As the Israelite farmer brought the first part of his harvest to the place of worship in gratitude, he recited these words of thanksgiving:

❝My ancestor was a wandering Aramean, a homeless refugee, who took his family to Egypt to live. They were few in number when they went there, but they became a large and powerful nation.

The Egyptians treated us harshly and forced us to work as slaves. Then we cried out for help to the Lord, the God of our ancestors. He heard us and

The Law today

How should we see the Old Testament Law today?
It is not a matter of keeping every smallest detail, on the grounds that 'rules is rules'. That is what the Jews tried to do after the exile. It led them into legalism – that is, the idea that you can earn God's favour by strictly keeping the rules. That can lead to self-righteousness and pride, as the apostle Paul found.
But neither is it a matter of ignoring the

Law, on the grounds that Jesus has fulfilled it, or that it only applied to the nation of Israel. So how should Christians treat the Law now?
We can look for the great moral principles that lie behind all the laws. Then we can start to work them out in our own lives, with the help of the Holy Spirit.
Sometimes the moral point of a law is very clear. We do not have to puzzle out what 'You shall not steal', or 'You shall not commit murder'

mean! But we should not think that there is a small category of moral laws which is all we need to bother about. Rather, we should try to take a wide survey of all the laws, and see the moral principles working in them wherever possible.

saw our suffering, hardship, and misery.

By his great power and strength he rescued us from Egypt. He worked miracles and wonders, and caused terrifying things to happen. He brought us here and gave us this rich fertile land.

So now I bring to the Lord the first part of the harvest that he has given **me.** Deuteronomy 26:5–10 **"**

The land God still owned

Although God had given the land to Israel, as proof of his love and faithfulness, in another sense it was still his land. It was as if he was the great landlord, and they were his tenants.

That was how the Canaanites before Israel had organized their economic system. The kings of the little city-states owned all the land and the people were tenant farmers. But in Israel God owned the land, so it was to him that the people owed loyalty.

66 'The land is mine', said God 'and you are my guests and tenants.' **99**

Leviticus 25:23

So what did this mean in practice? God was concerned about everything that was done with the land. He cared about how it was shared out, what was done with its produce, how those who worked on it

God talk

The Old Testament talks about God by using language which normally applies only to human beings. God sees, hears, speaks, remembers, is pleased or angry, laughs and shouts. He has hands and fingers, arms, a heart, feet, and a throne. The Old Testament writers often use human language to describe God.

Some people regard this as primitive and childish. They believe that this way of thinking about God is unnecessary or misleading. But this is not true:

● **It is metaphorical.** When the Bible writers used this kind of language, they knew they were not talking literally. They knew that God is spirit. He has no physical form and cannot be seen.

● **It is God's choice.** God made us in his own likeness, so it is natural that we should use language that describes ourselves to speak about him. It is the highest form of language, not the lowest, because it is personal rather than abstract. It is no disrespect to God to use human terms about him, as long as we remember that he is greater than any description. Jesus used human terms about God all the time.

● **It reminds us that God is alive and personal.** God is not an object or an idea. It is because he is the living God that we can speak of him as of a living man. He is a person.

All that we regard as precious about our own human personhood is infinitely true of God, for our personality derives from his. This is important, because it is what enables us to have a meaningful relationship with God.

You cannot love, trust or obey a principle or a force. The more abstract God becomes, the less we can know him as a person. The Bible emphasizes this by using human terms about him.

And, of course, in order to prove the point, God went beyond mere words and became human himself. God's last word, Jesus his Son, was in the most human language possible.

(human and animal) were treated. The whole of Israel's economic life had a religious and moral aspect.

This explains a number of features in the Old Testament:

● **It explains why there are so many laws in the Old Testament about the use of the land.** There are laws fixing proper boundaries, how to deal with disputes, who pays for damages, and so on. These were all part of the very down-to-earth responsibility of living as God's people on God's land.

● **It explains why disputes over land were so heated.** The best example of this is the story of Naboth in 1 Kings 21. He was killed because he would not sell his land to King Ahab. He regarded it as given by God to his family and he had a right to it and a responsiblity for it.

● **It explains why the prophets got so indignant about the economic and social injustice they saw.** People were being driven off their own land, because they could not pay their debts to the rich who callously oppressed them. A family that lost its land lost the biggest single thing which enabled them to feel and enjoy the blessing of God. It made them feel cut off from the true people of God.

God promised to give his homeless people a fertile land of their own – the promised land.

● **It explains why the worst judgement which God eventually brought on his people for their sin was to drive them out of his land altogether into exile.**

After a couple of generations, he brought them back again to his land. This too was another symbolic proof that he had forgiven his people and restored the relationship between them.

PASSAGES TO READ

4

STRUGGLE FOR SURVIVAL

The history of Israel could be described as a story of survival against the odds. For centuries the question was whether they could survive long enough to take possession of Canaan.

Pharaoh had tried his exterminatory birth-control programme on them. The wilderness and other enemies had done their worst. But they survived and the land became theirs. Now the question was, could they survive in the land itself? For two centuries after the death of Joshua, the nation seemed doomed to fall apart internally or to be destroyed by invaders from outside. This period is known as the time of the Judges.

The names of most of these early leaders of Israel are pretty obscure. But at least one has found his way into the popular Hall of Fame of folk heroes – Samson, with his enormous strength, his long hair, his tumultuous love affair with Delilah and his (literally) crashing farewell performance.

The Book of Judges can be exciting reading, but it also has a lot to teach us, as we look behind the scenes.

DISUNITY

For a long time the tribes of Israel were engaged in their own private struggles:

● They struggled to hold on to and expand the territory they had captured from the Canaanites.

● They got cut off from each other by the mountains and valleys of the country.

● They were also separated by parts of the country where Canaanites still held control or where other nations invaded.

● They had no capital city, no king or central leadership, no national standing army.

● On top of their internal problems, there was repeated pressure from outside as they were attacked or invaded by various foreign nations.

Yet still they managed to hold on to a sense of unity in two ways, both of which had practical effects.

● **They had a common sense of being Israel.** They belonged to one another and had a moral obligation to come to each other's help. This is illustrated by the story of Gideon, who mobilized an army from the different tribes before setting out to defeat the Midianites.

● **They also remembered that they were the people of God.** The battles they fought to survive were regarded as God's wars against his enemies. He was their real king, superior to the local leaders. And although the tribes developed their own customs and traditions, there was a common focus of worship of God at the religious centre of Shiloh. There, the ark of the covenant was kept.

DISLOYALTY

The Book of Judges is rather depressing because it records how Israel repeatedly turned away from wholehearted obedience to God. Even though they claimed to be the people of God, they began to worship the gods of the previous inhabitants of the land.

As a result, God allowed them to be invaded, until in despair they turned back to him again and pleaded for his deliverance. The whole story reads like a giant historical see-saw.

It can be very easy for us to condemn Israel and wonder how they could have been disloyal so frequently. We find it hard to believe that they didn't learn their lesson. But we need to understand how they were tempted to think.

The people of Israel had to spend many years fighting a guerilla war against the enemies they had only half-defeated.

● The worship of Baal must have seemed very natural. After all, he was the god of the land they had taken over. And the inhabitants of the land had obviously found him to be very reliable. Look at their successes in agriculture, commerce, civilization!

● Israel was pretty inexperienced in trading and farming when they invaded the land. This was hardly surprising after being slaves in Egypt and then wandering in the wilderness for a generation. So they thought that while they would keep worshipping Yahweh, surely there was no harm in roping in the help of the gods of their new land as well.

● Baal was reckoned to be the god of rain, fertility and crops, of a successful sex life, of business and commerce. In other words, he was the god of everything that seemed to matter in a practical way.

● As for God, sure, he was great in wartime, and it was so reassuring to have him on our side. But he was a bit

Israel's judges were like national heroes. They were popular because they humiliated and defeated the nation's enemies.

too strict and cramping, and too remote for real life. For everyday, practical affairs you needed Baal. Or so it seemed.

Perhaps they weren't so very different from some modern-day people who claim to be Christians. They reckon God is OK now and then, for Sundays or at least at Christmans and Easter. And certainly it's good if he is on our side in wartime.

But they spend most of their everyday lives worshipping other gods. They don't worship Baal, but all the idols of modern man. Success, power, money, position, technology and so on. God seems quite remote from the things that really matter in life.

But such an attitude and way of life is a betrayal of God – for us, just as much as for the Israelites. For God wants to be Lord of the whole of our lives, not just a comfortably religious bit. And if we try to mix other gods alongside him, we will find, as the Israelites did, that there is no peace or unity in our lives.

DELIVERANCE

What stands out in the Book of Judges is not so much the repeated failures of Israel as the great acts of God in delivering them. To do this he used some heroic figures, called the judges. Who were these leaders who delivered Israel, and why were they called judges?

● **They were called to their work by God.** They were not self-appointed – some of them were very reluctant heroes indeed! Nor were they democratically elected by the people. It was God who took the initiative, as we have seen before.

They were God's special agents. They acted on his behalf, carrying out his plans, exercising his authority. There was no full-time king at this period because God was seen to be the real king of the people. When the judges won a victory, it was God's victory, because God was acting through them.

● **They were called judges because they carried out God's justice.** We tend to think of a judge as someone who presides in a court of law to punish criminals and arbitrate in disputes. Certainly that was part of the work of some of the judges at this time.

But the scope of God's justice was wider than merely legal matters. If his people were being oppressed and downtrodden, then there was injustice. So when he raised up leaders to defeat and drive out these invading enemies, it was regarded as an act of justice – God's justice.

● **They acted in the power of God's Spirit.** There was nothing very special about any of them as individuals. They were not part of a royal dynasty, and they were not superhuman. They were special because the Spirit of God acted in them and gave them authority to lead.

Gideon is the best example of this. He protested that he was weak and insignificant. But God answered him, 'You can do it, because I will help you.' Later we read, 'The Spirit of the Lord took control of Gideon'. Literally this means, 'The Spirit of God clothed himself with Gideon'.

When Israel was ruled by a king, he was anointed with oil, which symbolized the Spirit of God. This showed that they were filled with the power and presence of God to do his will.

● **They were examples of faith.** The writer of the letter to the Hebrews in the New Testament includes some of the judges in his list of heroes of faith in chapter 11.

This is not because they were shining figures of untarnished virtue. Some of them were rather unsavoury characters, and even the best had moments of weakness and sin. But they trusted God and obeyed him even against impossible odds. And that really, at its simplest, is what faith is.

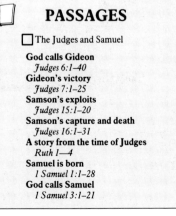

PASSAGES

☐ The Judges and Samuel

God calls Gideon
Judges 6:1–40
Gideon's victory
Judges 7:1–25
Samson's exploits
Judges 15:1–20
Samson's capture and death
Judges 16:1–31
A story from the time of Judges
Ruth 1—4
Samuel is born
1 Samuel 1:1–28
God calls Samuel
1 Samuel 3:1–21

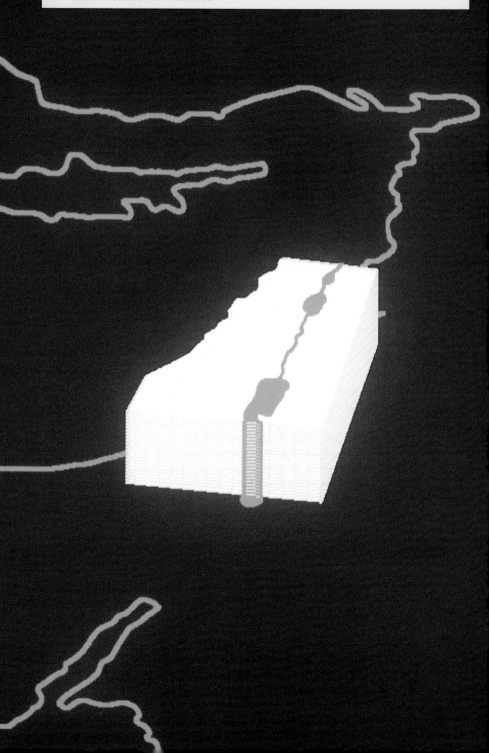

THREE KINGS

The story of the little shepherd boy who felled the Philistine giant with a single stone is universally popular. But it is not just a good story. It was a key event in the next period of Israel's history. This was the time of the first three kings of Israel.

The event took place during the reign of Saul, but the young David had already been anointed secretly as the next king. In Saul, it sowed the seeds of a jealousy that became murderous, insane, and eventually suicidal.

But it showed up in David two big qualities – trust in God, and personal courage. These qualities won him the kingdom which he handed on to his son Solomon.

Saul, David and Solomon ruled over all the tribes of Israel. It was a century that completely transformed the nation.

WHY DID ISRAEL WANT A KING?

Israel did not become a monarchy overnight. The change-over from the judges to the kings was slow. At the end of the period of the judges, Israel had a new leader, called Samuel. Samuel exercised a leadership that was almost like a king in some ways, while Saul (the first king) was similar to the preceding judges.

However, between Samuel and Saul there was a definite break. There came a point when the people demanded to have a real king. But what was it that led up to this change?

Samuel's leadership

Samuel was an outstanding man of God

The events recorded in the Bible happened on the crossroads of the continents, at the eastern end of the Mediterranean.

who bridged the gap between the period of the judges and the monarchy. He was a legal judge himself, as well as being a successful military leader. He also functioned as a priest and as a prophet.

He seems to have been greatly loved and respected by the people. But sadly, he was never able to overcome the attacks made on Israel by their neighbours, the Philistines. And in his old age his own sons let him down. They did not follow his example. Instead, they gave in to the temptations of bribery and corruption.

This was one of the things that led to the people asking for a king. They thought this would give them a more permanent and stable form of leadership.

The Philistines

These were the worst of any of the enemies that the tribes of Israel had had to face. They were a fierce people with an alien culture who had settled on the western coastal plain of Palestine. They used superior weapons, including chariots.

They treated Israel's tribesmen with contempt. The Philistines not only beat them in battle, but stole the ark of the covenant as well.

The Israelites were deeply humiliated. They began to feel that their only hope lay in a strong, unified front, under the leadership of a permanent king.

Popular demand

The representatives of the people came to Samuel and asked him to appoint a king for them. We can see the pressures that gave rise to the request, but it did not please Samuel at all. There were two reasons for this:

● **Like the other nations.** The people said they wanted a king so that they would be like the other nations. But God had called them to be different from other nations. They were to be his own, holy people. Samuel knew that kingship would bring with it all sorts of evil that they would come to regret.

● **Dissatisfaction with God's rule.** The people wanted a human king because they were dissatisfied with the direct rule of God and the leaders he had raised up in time of need. God said to Samuel, 'I am the one they have rejected as their king.' Like their worship of other gods, it was another sign of their disloyalty and lack of faith in God.

GOD'S RESPONSE

God gave them a king as they asked. Indeed, he and Samuel went to considerable trouble in choosing Saul, anointing him and persuading him to be king. The desire came from the people, but the choice was God's.

Samuel left the people in no doubt about what they would suffer if the king of Israel really did behave like the kings of other nations. He warned them that they would suffer all kinds of financial and social loss, through taxation, forced labour, confiscation, and so on. As it turned out in later centuries, his warnings came grimly true.

Israel's request for a king was sinful. The monarchy failed to live up to the people's expectations. But in spite of this, God promised to bless the king and the nation, as long as they both obeyed him. But if they disobeyed, both people and king would suffer his judgement.

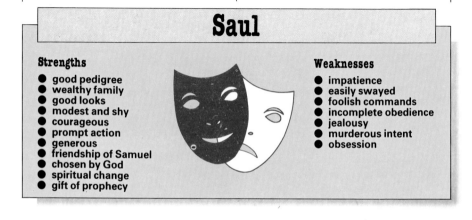

Saul

Strengths
● good pedigree
● wealthy family
● good looks
● modest and shy
● courageous
● prompt action
● generous
● friendship of Samuel
● chosen by God
● spiritual change
● gift of prophecy

Weaknesses
● impatience
● easily swayed
● foolish commands
● incomplete obedience
● jealousy
● murderous intent
● obsession

This meant that the king himself was just as much subject to God and his Law as any other Israelite. He was not above the Law. He was certainly not divine himself (as some other countries regarded their kings). On the contrary, he was to set an example to his people in observing the Law of the covenant.

So kingship in Israel got under way, with a double-sided aspect to it. It came about through human motives that were impure. But at the same time the kingship was given by God. And the king remained very much under the superior authority of God.

KING SAUL

The first king of Israel was as double-sided as the office he took on. He had many gifts and made some successful achievements. But there were fatal weaknesses in his character which led him to disaster. His reign ended with the Israelites more firmly under the Philistines than they had been before.

As a result, Saul is one of the greatest tragic figures of the Bible. The story of his life and death, entangled with the story of the rise of David, occupies the rest of the Book of 1 Samuel. It is a superb piece of storytelling. It is worth reading as a whole just for the sake of its excellent writing, apart from the moral and spiritual content.

In the end, Saul came to a shattering awareness of his own folly. He experienced such intense loneliness that he was driven to seek help from the dead Samuel through a medium – a practice which he himself had prohibited.

In utter exhaustion, he finally took his own life as the Israelites were defeated at the battle of Mount Gilboa. They had asked for a king to drive out the Philistines. As their first king died, they were more under the Philistine heel than ever.

KING DAVID

David had many of the same sort of advantages as Saul. But in his early years, as a shepherd boy, and later on the run from Saul, his qualities were tested and strengthened.

He learned patience and wisdom. He had the ability to lead people by tact as well as strength. Above all he learned what it meant to trust in God in the midst of impossible circumstances and in danger of life itself.

Because of his humility and obedience, he is described as 'a man after God's own heart'.

When Saul died there was a struggle for the throne. Abner (Saul's former commander-in-chief) tried to set up Saul's remaining son, Ishbosheth, as king. But David had already been acclaimed as king at Hebron in the territory of his own tribe, Judah. After a nasty civil war, Ishbosheth was murdered, and David was acknowledged by all the tribes.

David ruled for seven years at Hebron. But then he took a step which was to have great significance for the rest of human history. He captured Jerusalem and made it the capital of his kingdom.

Strategically, it was a superb choice. It was fairly central, and was easily fortified and defended as it was on a hill. David built himself a palace there and made it the centre of his political administration of the state.

He also brought the ark of the covenant into Jerusalem, amid great popular rejoicing. Jerusalem became not only 'The City of David', but Zion, 'The City of God'. It was the focal point for the faith of the tribes of Israel.

With his capital secure, David went on to consolidate his own kingdom. He organized it internally, with a system of government and administration. And he protected it externally by conquering most of the surrounding nations and making them pay taxes and tribute to him.

For the first time since their arrival, the Israelites were in control of the whole of the land that had been promised to Abraham.

The Bible is utterly frank and honest about even its greatest heroes. It does not paint them in glowing colours, but shows their weaknesses and failures too.

David fell into a web of sin that included adultery, deception and planned murder. The experience brought a very sharp response from God through a prophet called Nathan. David deeply repented and was forgiven, but the consequences of his sin poisoned his own family life.

He lacked the moral authority to prevent one of his sons behaving in a similar way. The final years of his reign were torn apart with civil war within his own family. Even as he was dying there was bloodshed over who would succeed him. Eventually David died at the age of seventy and the throne passed to Solomon.

KING SOLOMON

Solomon was a great and glorious king, internationally renowned for his wisdom and wealth. His long reign with no wars gave Israel a period of peace such as they had never known before – or would again.

However, like Saul, his reign was a mixture of good and evil. The details of Solomon's life and rule can be found in 1 Kings 3–11.

By the end of Solomon's reign, the people resented the Jerusalem court and its ways. The worst of Samuel's prediction of the way a king might behave had come sadly true.

The northern tribes especially disliked being ruled from the south. Shortly after Solomon's death, they rebelled and split off to form their own kingdom. The united monarchy and the great days of an Israelite empire were at an end.

Solomon

The Good

- He built the temple.
- He encouraged culture through international contact with other civilizations.
- He extended Israel's trade and the nation became prosperous.
- He improved the administration system and fortified some defensive cities.

The Bad

- He antagonized the northern tribes.
- He endangered Israel's faith through foreign marriages and political alliances.
- His policies created the bad effects of rich merchants, poor peasants.
- His heavy taxes and forced labour led to bitterness.

King Solomon's many wives were a symbol of his great wealth. He had as many wives as some rich people today have cars . . .

PASSAGES TO READ

DIVIDED WE FALL

Double vision is very confusing. The next section of Old Testament history can seem confusing for the same reason. Israel was split into two separate kingdoms – Judah in the south and Israel in the north. This can make the story difficult to follow.

Kings keep overlapping, and some have the same name in different kingdoms. Sometimes they are at war with each other. Sometimes they are allies against some other enemy.

In the end both kingdoms are conquered. Then we find God's people right back where we found them before the exodus from Egypt – in slavery in a foreign land. Has God still any future for them?

THE SPLIT

In the later years of Solomon's reign, there was a lot of pent-up bitterness and frustration against the burden he was laying on the people. A northerner named Jeroboam led a rebellion against the Jerusalem monarchy. He had been an official in charge of Solomon's forced labour gangs.

The split occurred when the new king, Rehoboam, came to power. Jeroboam led the ten northern tribes in revolt, leaving Rehoboam with the two tribes of Judah and Benjamin. Jeroboam was made king of the northern kingdom, which took to itself the name Israel. The hostile division between north and south was never healed.

The two kingdoms developed very differently.
● **Politically, Judah was much more stable.** The monarchy passed from father to son with a descendant of David always on the throne (apart from one short break). Israel was more unstable. The throne was often claimed by the strongest contestant. There were frequent revolutions and power struggles.
● **Religiously, it was a similar story.** Judah was more conservative, with its solid basis of Jerusalem and the temple. Israel was more exposed to foreign nations and their religious influence. They had no central religious shrine. The northern kings were less faithful to God than those in Judah.

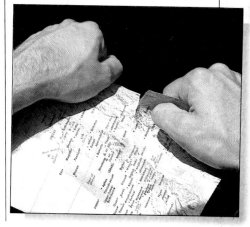

Elijah and Elisha

Elijah's name summed up his life's work. It means 'Yahweh is God'. His whole mission was to bring Israel back to see that Yahweh was the true and living God – not Baal.

His first act was to confront King Ahab with God's judgement. Because of the sin of the king and his people, the land would suffer a drought that would last three years.

At the end of this three years, Elijah arranged a dramatic showdown between himself and the prophets of Baal on Mount Carmel. Elijah (single-handed) versus the rest. God versus Baal.

It was a fantastic contest with a fiery and bloody end. It proved to the people who was the real God and brought them back to him.

Elijah was also concerned about social evil. He opposed Ahab for his treatment of Naboth, and said he would die because of it.

Elisha was trained by Elijah to take over from him. His name was significant too. It means 'God saves'.

During his long ministry as a prophet (it lasted fifty years, through the reigns of six kings), God worked many miracles through him. He healed the sick, fed the hungry, raised the dead and delivered whole cities from siege.

Jesus said that John the Baptist was like Elijah. Like Elijah, John called the people to repentance. And just as Elisha followed Elijah, so Jesus followed John.

Interestingly, the name Jesus means the same as Elisha in Hebrew: 'The Lord saves'. Many of Jesus' miracles were like scaled-up versions of those of Elisha.

Elijah and Elisha were not afraid to denounce the evil they saw among God's people. God was with them, and they often performed spectacular miracles.

● **Socially, the injustice and oppression that began under Solomon was felt in both kingdoms alike.** Attacking that oppression was a concern shared by the prophets of north and south.

THE KINGS OF ISRAEL

After the death of Jeroboam there was a constant struggle for power. A succession of kings ruled, one of whom only lasted for seven days!

● **Omri** became king and brought some stability to Israel. He bought a hill and built the city of Samaria on it for his capital. He made Israel an important nation in the power politics of the area. But already Israel was declining spiritually and morally.

● **Ahab** (Omri's son) married Jezebel. She was a Phoenician princess who was fanatically devoted to the Canaanite god Baal. She tried to wipe out the worship of God and replace it with Baal worship. Also, where Jezebel came from, the king was used to getting his own way. Common people didn't count for much. This now began to happen in Israel, despite the laws of Israel, which said that a king was not to lord it over the people.

 Two of the greatest prophets lived at this time. They were called Elijah and Elisha.

 Elijah prophesied a violent end for Ahab and Jezebel. Ahab met his end in battle. Jezebel was eventually killed in a bloody revolution led by Jehu.

● **Jeroboam II** enjoyed a long and prosperous reign. He recovered all Israel's lost territory. He brought wealth and luxury to his court at Samaria and to the wealthy upper class. Religion prospered too. It seemed that God and Israel were getting on fine together, to each other's mutual advantage.

But beneath the surface, the poor were getting poorer and were being driven off their own land by debts. But who could be bothered to look beneath the surface when everything seemed rosy? God's answer to that question was a shepherd from the south called Amos.

 Amos was sickened by what he saw in Israel. People flocked to the religious festivals, claiming to be serving God. Yet at the same time they were cheating the poor and perverting justice.

 Amos exposed their hypocrisy in stinging words. He said that God's judgement would fall on the nation. He predicted that Israel would be destroyed and the people carried off into exile.

 This was shocking and sounded like treason to the king. Amos was told bluntly to shut up and get out.

● **The fall of Israel.** They may have silenced Amos, but they could not stop God's punishment. In the twenty-five years after the death of Jeroboam II the nation simply fell apart.

 Samaria was besieged, captured and destroyed by the Assyrians. The Israelites of the northern tribes were taken into exile and scattered throughout the Assyrian Empire.

 The northern kingdom was finished. There were no more kings, and the people never returned from exile.

 Foreign people settled in Israelite territory. They intermarried with those Israelites who were left in the land, and produced the mixed race known as the Samaritans. So the split between Jews and Samaritans (referred to in Jesus' time) began.

THE KINGS OF JUDAH

After Solomon's kingdom was split, Israel and Judah were in conflict with each other for some time.

● **Uzziah** ruled Judah when

Hosea

Hosea lived at about the same time as the prophet Amos. His message was mainly for the northern kingdom, but he also had things to say to Judah. God's message to him came by way of bitter experience – as with several of the prophets. He married a woman called Gomer, who later was unfaithful to him. Hosea saw in his broken marriage a picture of the broken relationship between Israel and God. He spoke about the pain that Israel's unfaithfulness was causing God.

Yet Hosea was commanded to buy his former wife back from her life of prostitution, and to love her again. In this incredible act of love he symbolized God's faithfulness to his own people. He would not completely destroy them – there would be judgement, but beyond that lay the hope of restoration and a new relationship of love and faithfulness.

Hosea shows us a side of God's character that many people wrongly think is missing from the Old Testament – his loving tenderness, his desire to forgive, and his longing for an intimate relationship with his people.

Hosea had some painful things to say to Israel, but he also offered hope. God would bring peace and good harvests to the nation once again.

Amos

Amos was a great preacher who knew how to draw crowds. His first sermon was like a superb geography lesson. He proclaimed God's judgement on each of Israel's neighbours in turn, for the atrocities they had committed. Each of his attacks on Israel's enemies must have drawn loud cheers from the crowds.

'God will punish Syria!. . . the Philistines!. . . the Phoenicians!. . . Edom!. . . Ammon!. . . Moab!. . . Judah! Perhaps at the mention of Judah, the cheers died away a bit. Who could be next? Amos had skilfully drawn a noose of nations around Israel. There was nowhere left for God's judgement to fall but on themselves.

And sure enough, Israel was next. Amos struck home.

'This is what the Lord says: "For three sins of Israel, even for four, I will not turn back my wrath. They sell the righteous for silver, and the needy for a pair of sandals. They trample on the heads of the poor as upon the dust of the ground, and deny justice to the oppressed."' (Amos 2:6–7)

This was followed by a history lesson. Amos reminded the people of all that God had done for them. He had brought them out of Egypt and given them the land. But they were trampling on all of that. Soon God would trample on them in judgement, unless they repented and returned to justice again. God wanted justice in the courts, justice in the market places.

Amos was the first of the prophets who had his preaching written down and collected into a book. His message has a timeless relevance. God demands social justice among all people. He will not accept the worship of those who oppress or neglect the poor and downtrodden.

*'Let justice flow like a stream,
and righteousness like a river
that never goes dry.'*
Amos 5:24

Jeroboam II ruled Israel. This was a time of prosperity for the southern kingdom. Uzziah extended the borders of Judah, subdued surrounding nations, and reopened the port of Elath to trade. His power and prosperity recalled the great days of Solomon.

But power leads to pride and this led to Uzziah's downfall. He tried to take over the exclusive role of the priesthood, and was afflicted with leprosy in punishment. This was startling judgement on the arrogance that marred an otherwise godly reign.

● **Ahaz** ruled Judah at the time of Israel's fall to Assyria. During his reign, the northern kingdom of Israel formed an alliance with Syria to fight off the Assyrians. They invited Judah to join them. When Judah refused, they both turned to attack Judah instead.

Ahaz panicked and instead of trusting God, as Isaiah urged him to, he took the most incredibly foolish step. He invited Assyria to become Judah's ally against the other two nations. It was like bringing a lion into the house to catch a mouse!

As an ally of Assyria, Judah was forced to pay very heavy taxes. Ahaz introduced Assyrian idols, altars and rituals into the temple of Jerusalem. Judah became a satellite state, under the rule of Assyria.

● **Hezekiah** (who followed Ahaz as king) rejected the Assyrian domination. He reversed Ahaz's policy, cleansed Jerusalem of pagan cults, and then rebelled against Assyria.

This courageous stand brought immediate action from Assyria. They were not used to insults from petty kingdoms. The Assyrian king Sennacherib led his forces into Judah and devastated the country. He captured all the fortified cities, except Jerusalem.

Hezekiah did the right thing. He turned over the whole desperate situation to God. Isaiah gave him God's answer: 'Assyria will be punished. They will leave without firing an arrow. Jerusalem will be safe.'

God kept his word. Most of Sennacherib's army was annihilated (probably by a plague) and Sennacherib withdrew in a hurry. God had shown his mighty power to save his people.

● **Josiah** was a later king who began his reign at the age of eight. During his long reign the giant of Assyria at last over-reached itself. It could no longer hold its vast empire together by sheer force of terror, and so it collapsed. Babylon rose to replace Assyria as the dominant world power.

Josiah took advantage of this changeover and reasserted Judah's independence. At the same time he pursued a more dramatic course of reform than any previous king.

All the shrines, idols and altars from foreign nations were destroyed. The temple itself was repaired and cleaned. During these repairs, an old scroll was discovered by workmen. It turned out to be the book of the Law (which probably included Deuteronomy). Josiah read it and was distressed to realize that God's Law had not been kept. But he was also encouraged to carry on with his reforms.

During Josiah's reign God called another young man to be his prophet. His name was Jeremiah. He worked as a prophet until the tragic days of Jerusalem's total destruction by the Babylonians.

● **Zedekiah** was the last king of Judah. He rebelled against the power of Babylon, as a previous king had done ten years earlier. King Nebuchadnezzar of Babylon threw his whole angry weight against Jerusalem.

The siege lasted two years until starvation destroyed the people and Babylonian battering rams destroyed the walls. The army of Judah fled, but they were captured and killed. Zedekiah watched his sons being put to death, and then his eyes were put out.

Large numbers of people and vast quantities of wealth were carried off to exile in Babylon. The whole of the city was burned to the ground. Solomon's beautiful 400-year-old temple and the city walls were reduced to rubble.

The horror of it all is almost unimaginable. The book of Lamentations, and Psalm 137 give us an insight into what the people of Israel felt. They watched the very pillars of their nation and faith go up in smoke. They were forced to leave behind the land God had so miraculously given them centuries ago.

Where was their God now? Could he really be doing this to his own people? Was it his hand behind the fist of Nebuchadnezzar? Or was he really powerless? They had always trusted God because of what he had done in the past. But how could they cope with the present when it seemed to be the end of the story? Could there be any future for them after this?

These were the burning questions that faced the exiles as they trudged to faraway Babylon. They were to have fifty years to find the answers. Fifty years of exile. A whole generation learned again what it was to be strangers in a foreign land, waiting for God.

PASSAGES TO READ

☐ **Kings of Israel**

The northern revolt
1 Kings 12:1–33
Jeroboam and Rehoboam
1 Kings 14:1–31
Introducing Elijah
1 Kings 17:1–24
Elijah confronts Ahab
1 Kings 18:1–19
God v Baal
1 Kings 18:20–46
Elijah and Elisha
1 Kings 19:1–21
The murder of Naboth
1 Kings 21:1–29

☐ **Israel goes into Exile**

Elijah taken to heaven
2 Kings 2:1–18
Elisha's miracles
2 Kings 4:1–37
Elisha heals Naaman
2 Kings 5:1–27
King Ahaz calls Assyria
2 Chronicles 28:1–27
The fall of Samaria
2 Kings 17:1–23
Assyria attacks Jerusalem
2 Kings 18:1–37
Hezekiah trusts God
2 Kings 19:1–37

☐ **Judah goes into Exile**

Hezekiah's illness
2 Kings 20:1–11
King Josiah
2 Kings 22:1–20
Josiah eliminates paganism
2 Kings 23:1–37
Jerusalem falls
2 Kings 25:1–17
Judah goes into exile
2 Kings 25:18–30
Sorrow over ruined Jerusalem
Lamentations 2:1–22
Praying for God's mercy
Lamentations 5:1–22

☐ **Amos and Hosea**

Verdict on the nations
Amos 1:1—3:2
Turn back to God!
Amos 5:1–24
Doom for Israel
Amos 8:1–14
God's marriage to Israel
Hosea 1:1—2:1
Israel's adultery
Hosea 2:2—3:5
Worshipping other gods
Hosea 4:1–14
Hope for Israel
Hosea 14:1–9

☐ **Selections from Isaiah**

Jerusalem is warned
Isaiah 1:1–20
God's peace, human pride
Isaiah 2:1–22
Song of the Vineyard
Isaiah 5:1–30
God calls Isaiah
Isaiah 6:1–13
Isaiah's message to Ahaz
Isaiah 7:1–25
Assyria, God's stick
Isaiah 10:5–27
The land of peace
Isaiah 11:1–9

☐ **Selections from Jeremiah**

God calls Jeremiah
Jeremiah 1:1–19
Jeremiah in the temple
Jeremiah 7:1–15
The potter
Jeremiah 18:1–12
Jeremiah's anguish
Jeremiah 20:7–18; 4:19–22
Two kinds of figs
Jeremiah 24:1–10
A new covenant
Jeremiah 31:1–34
Jeremiah thrown into a well
Jeremiah 38:1–28

Isaiah

Isaiah is a prince among the prophets. He probably came from a noble family. He seems to have spent his whole career in Jerusalem, with easy access to the royal court. He was a respected adviser to some kings and a fierce critic of others.

Isaiah had a lofty vision of the holiness, majesty and power of God. Because of this he was bitterly opposed to all forms of human arrogance – whether he found it in the rulers of his own country, or in the military taunts of the Assyrian Empire.

His main message was that Judah should trust in God in the face of the international pressures of the time. Judah should not run off to make useless alliances with other nations. But he was often disappointed when the rulers rejected his advice. They refused to believe God alone could save them. And like Israel, the poor were unjustly treated by the rich.

Isaiah compared Judah to a vine that had been carefully cultivated by its owner, only to produce wild and bitter grapes.

Isaiah predicted that the nation would suffer God's judgement through defeat in war and exile. But he also saw beyond the judgement to a glorious age when God's people would live in justice and peace. There would be a new son of David, the Messiah. All the nations of the world would be ruled by him and follow the ways of God.

Some of these great prophecies are taken up by the New Testament and applied to Jesus in his first coming. Others will clearly only be fulfilled when he comes again finally to establish his kingdom.

The Middle East today is a place of tension, political disputes and violence. It was the same in the time of Isaiah the prophet: the people feared invasion.

STATE SECURITY REPORT

Reporting Officer

Name of subject	Jeremiah (son of Hilkiah)
Tribe	Benjamin
Occupation	Prophet (of doom)
Age last birthday	58
Background	Comes from a family of priests living north of Jerusalem
Career	Claims to have been called by God to be a prophet when he was in his twenties. His messages are bitter attacks on the people of Jerusalem. In particular: 1. During the reign of King Josiah, the king himself reformed and strengthened our faith. But Jeremiah said that people's hearts were not changed. He compared the reforms to soft soap that only touched the surface. 2. He continues to attack the belief held by many people that Jerusalem can never be captured by our enemies. He says that because the nation has disobeyed God, the city will be destroyed. This is treason!
Any previous convictions	1. Arrested, beaten and chained all night for preaching about the fall of Jerusalem. 2. Imprisoned by order of King Zedekiah for preaching treason. 3. Thrown into a deep well for saying that the Babylonians would capture Jerusalem.
Recommendations	Get this man out of the country!

TOP SECRET

What's in it for us?

We have finished our survey of the turbulent centuries between Solomon and the exile. Now we can step back a bit and find out what the Bible has to say to us now:

● **God controls what goes on.** The prophets said that God is actually in charge of all that happens in the international world of power politics. Isaiah said that Assyria (the most fearsome world power at the time) was nothing more than a stick in God's hand. He would quickly throw the stick away as soon as he had done his work!

It is amazing that those who wrote this lived at a time when the gods of these great empires seemed to have triumphed. Yet they wrote with the same conviction: God is in control!

Christians in the modern world need to remind themselves of this unshakeable Old Testament belief.

● **God's demand is social as well as personal.** We tend to think of religion as an individual and private matter. But the message of Israel's history is that God is concerned about society too. He demands justice in the law courts and honesty in trade.

Above all, he cares for the poor and the weak. He cares for those who are defenceless –

especially widows, orphans, the landless and immigrant strangers. All of this has a direct challenge to us today.

● **Politics matter.** Those who have authority of any kind in a nation are God's special concern. He holds them responsible for the state of society. He cares about their political activity.

The historical books of this period are full of politics. There are economic policies and military strategies. There are protest movements and revolutions. And there is public spending, taxation, espionage and diplomacy.

All of it comes under God's gaze, and under his criticism through the prophets. Politics clearly matter very much to God.

● **Prophets suffer.** Those who brought the message of God to the nation suffered for it. They were up against those who rejected God and preferred to go their own arrogant way. People who dared to criticize them paid a heavy price: unpopularity, contempt, isolation, and sometimes death. The Christian church follows in the footsteps of the prophets and Jesus too. When it brings the challenge of the Bible to society, then it will suffer as they did.

● **Privilege means greater responsibility.** When disaster fell, some Jews asked why God was doing this to them. After all, they were his special people.

He had done so much for them in the past. But God showed them that he expected great things from them because of what he had done. They had experienced his grace and power in being delivered from Egypt. He had given them a land to live in and law to live by. So they were even more to blame for their failure to obey him. This was why their punishment was so severe.

To belong to God's people is not an empty privilege. It makes us responsible to live as people for whom God has done great things.

● **Outward religion can be false security.** God had given his people all kinds of outward symbols and rituals to help their faith. There were the sacrifices, the festivals, and the temple.

The danger was that the people thought that by going through the religious rituals they could keep God happy. It did not matter what the rest of their lives and the state of society was like.

The prophets had to expose this delusion. The sacrifices of disobedient people were not pleasing to God. He was far more concerned with justice, compassion and humility than with outward ritual. This is still true for us.

*Bewildered at the destruction
of Jerusalem, the Jewish
people knew that their faith
could not survive without
God's special help.*

WAITING FOR GOD

Think of the length of time between Henry VIII and today. The time between the exile of the Jews in Babylon and the coming of Jesus Christ was a bit longer than that. Just over 500 years. The Old Testament only covers the first 150 years of that period. After Malachi (the last prophet of the Old Testament), the Jews lived on through many ups and downs. Another couple of empires came and went.

At last John the Baptist appeared, preaching that the kingdom of God was just around the corner. He was the first prophet to be heard in nearly 400 years. No wonder he caused a nationwide stir!

It had been a long wait. A time of great expectations and great frustrations. A time of great suffering and wild rebellions. A time of patient hope. Waiting for God.

THE EXILE

People react very differently to any kind of national calamity. Some are bitter. Some are broken. Some are defiant. Some look for a way up and out. The Jews were just the same after the horrific destruction of their homeland and their way of life.

● **Some turned their backs on God for good.** They thought that he had been shown to have no real power. Things had been better in the old days, when they had worshipped other gods.

This was the same as the reaction of the Jews under Moses in the desert. At the first sign of hardship, they wished they had never left Egypt.

● **Some accepted that what had happened was God's doing. But they complained bitterly that it was unjust and unfair.**

It was all the fault of previous generations, they said. They were being punished for the sins of their ancestors. The prophet Ezekiel had to show them that they were bearing their own guilt too.

● **Some accepted that it was God's doing, and that they had deserved it.** What had happened was his just judgement on their persistent sin. They had refused again and again to listen to his voice through the prophets.

These people were completely broken. To them, the exile could mean only one thing. God had cast them off. They could see no hope. There was no way back.

But even so, they cried out to God in desperation. As generations of their ancestors had done before them, they pleaded for mercy.

Because they turned back to God the prophets of the exile held out hope to them alone. Hope of forgiveness. Hope for a new future.

Ezekiel

The prophets were all unusual people, but Ezekiel was the most eccentric of them all! God called him to do some very strange things in order to get his word across to his people in very strange times.

Ezekiel was taken to Babylon as an exile before the final destruction of Jerusalem. Five years later he was called to be a prophet. His work as a prophet started before Jerusalem fell. It overlapped with the last years of Jeremiah's ministry in the royal prison in Jerusalem.

He used some strange visual aids to act out his message.

● He lay down to besiege a clay model of Jerusalem – portraying all the horrors of siege.
● He shaved off his hair. Then he burnt some, cut up some, and saved just a few strands. This symbolized the fate of God's people.
● He dug through the walls of his own home to portray the hurried escape of people in Jerusalem.
● When he lost his own wife, even that became a sign of the nation's grief and horror.

After he had received news that Jerusalem had fallen, the tone of his message changed to one of comfort and new hope for the people.

He looked forward to a new covenant, with a descendant of David on the throne. He would rule like a shepherd over his sheep in a time of blessing and peace.

His most famous vision is the 'Valley of Dry Bones' (Ezekiel 37). It gives a picture of Israel in exile. Under the miraculous power of God's Spirit, the bones come together, are reclothed in flesh, and come back to life! The restoration of Israel will be no less a miracle.

'Tell these dry bones to listen to the word of the Lord. Tell them that I, the Sovereign Lord, am saying to them: I am going to put breath into you and bring you back to life.'
Ezekiel 37:4–5

SURVIVAL KIT

The exile could have been the end of Israel altogether. Like so many of the other little nations conquered by the Assyrians and Babylonians, she could have been swallowed up and buried for ever in the sands of ancient history.

Even the faith of Israel was in danger of dying. The promised land lay desolate and nearly empty. The city of David and Solomon's temple were in ruins. All the sacrifices and festivals had ended. Their king, a descendant of David, was in a Babylonian prison.

Again, it was the prophets who came to the rescue. They gave Israel a survival kit for these difficult times. The main prophet was Ezekiel, who was a younger contemporary of Jeremiah.

Early in the exile they gave the people an interpretation of what had happened to them. They helped them come to terms with preserving their faith in a whole new world. Like so many prophets before them, they kept on insisting that the calamity of exile was God's judgement.

● **God's judgement was logical.** Sin deserved to be punished. That had been a central part of Israel's faith from the start. Their own legal system was based on it. Their history was full of examples of it. God had shattered the Egyptians for enslaving Israel. He had driven out the Canaanites for their abominable ways. And he had warned that he would do the same to Israel if they broke his laws.

Now the warnings God had given were being carried out. It showed that God really meant what he said.

● **God's judgement was limited.** While Israel's punishment was certainly deserved, it would come to an end. God promised that he would carry on with his original plan for his people. He told them that he would keep his promises as well as his threats.

RETURN FROM EXILE

The Assyrians and Babylonians had a policy of divide and conquer. It was brutal. It bred fear and terror. And it worked – for a while. Cyrus and the Persians were more in favour of conquer and unite.

The earlier empires had deliberately shifted populations around. They scattered them into exile. And they took their gods to their own capital cities to show how well and truly beaten they were.

While the Jews were in exile, a new empire (Persian) took over, ruled by King Cyrus. Cyrus believed it made much more sense to have the gods on his side. And he believed in returning captives to their own lands. There they would be grateful subjects, praying to their gods for him.

Cyrus's first act on conquering the territories of Babylon was to allow the captive peoples and their gods to return to their native lands. As far as the Jews were concerned, they believed that God had brought Cyrus to power for this very purpose.

But there was no mad rush to return. Many Jews remained in Babylon. They thought that the journey home was too long and dangerous. They knew how hard it would be to start life again. And anyway, many of them were comfortable in Babylon. They enjoyed success and wealth.

Yet thousands did go back in several waves. They did not go back to start up a new independent state of Judah. They were simply a tiny community within a corner of one of the big provinces of the Persian Empire.

The returning exiles faced a very tough situation:
● The land itself had been more or less neglected agriculturally for a generation.

Isaiah and the exiles

Towards the end of the exile, the promise of an end to punishment was spelt out more clearly. The prophecies contained in the second half of the book of Isaiah painted a glorious new picture of Israel's future and the majesty of God.

These chapters may have come originally from Isaiah himself (who lived before the exile began). Or they may have come from a different prophet who lived at the time of the exile whose name we do not know. But there is no doubt that they apply to the exiles on the eve of their return to Judah.

They are the most glorious chapters in the Old Testament. It is worth trying to read Isaiah 40–55 through at one go if possible, to feel their power.

The message they gave to the exiles was:
● **A new future.** The great message is that the past is now behind them. The punishment is over. God is about to do something new. He will do something greater than anything that had happened to them before.
● **A new exodus.** God will lead them out of slavery, just as he had led them out of Egypt. The prophecies contain rich imagery about the journey through the desert, and how God will provide for them.
● **A new revelation of God.** Like the first exodus, this new act of God would show people a thing or two about him. These chapters ring with the uniqueness of God.

He alone is the creator of the universe. He alone controls history from beginning to end. He alone can predict events and bring them about. He alone is the living God – there is no other.
● **A new covenant.** The people had broken the demands of the Sinai covenant, and had suffered its curses. But God would now fulfil his covenant with Abraham, to make his descendants a blessing to the whole world. So the new covenant would be the fulfilment of that promise.
● **A new hope for other nations.** Israel had always believed that they were called for the sake of other nations. But in practice they had been narrow and exclusive in their expression of God's relationship with them.

Now the full extent of God's plans are shown. He wants to be the deliverer of the whole world. God will work through Israel to deliver all people.

In exile, the Jewish people began to see the Old Testament scriptures as the most important aspect of their faith. They introduced 'synagogues' to teach and read the scriptures.

● Villages and towns and the city of Jerusalem itself were skeletons of their former busy life.

● They faced suspicion and opposition from the inhabitants of the northern territory.

● There were enormous problems with bad harvests and housing needs.

● They were also hindered by a campaign of political tale-telling against them.

The Jewish exiles had returned home. Now they faced the task of reconstructing not only their towns and their way of life, but also their faith in God.

Into this depressing scene God sent another batch of prophets. These were the last of the Old Testament spokesmen for God:

● **Haggai's** message was one of encouragement. He criticized the people for neglecting the building work on the temple. He called them to renew the work.

He is one of the few bright spots in the story of the prophets, for the people actually listened to him and did what he said. Perhaps this was something of a shock to him! So the temple was finished, and there were predictions of future glory and blessing.

● **Zechariah** preached at the same time as Haggai. He predicted glory for Jerusalem as a whole. He linked this with the arrival of its true king, the Messiah.

His messages were highly pictorial and symbolic. They include the vision of Israel's king riding into Jerusalem on a donkey – fulfilled by Jesus when he entered Jerusalem before his death.

● **Malachi** came later than Haggai and Zechariah. He was concerned that the people and their priests were becoming very lazy in their service of God.

They seemed to feel that God didn't care enough to help them. So why should they sacrifice the best of what they had to him? Malachi said they were actually robbing God with their miserable offerings and insincere worship. He warned them to change their ways and prepare for the day when God himself would come.

That day was still centuries away. But it was this last prophecy of Malachi that John the Baptist repeated. He too told people to repent and prepare for God's arrival.

EZRA AND NEHEMIAH

A generation went by. Persia was still very much the world empire. The temple had been rebuilt, but the people of Judah still lived in confusion.

They were in danger of being absorbed into the non-Jewish population. Jerusalem was still partly ruined and without walls. It was a disgrace to the God who was worshipped there.

Reconstruction was needed. Jerusalem's walls needed to be rebuilt. The people's faith needed to be strengthened.

This work of reconstruction fell to two men – Nehemiah and Ezra. They had both risen to positions of high office within the Persian civil service. At different times they were both given permission to go to Jerusalem. They went with the Persian king's authority to organize affairs there.

Nehemiah's great achievement was the building of the walls of Jerusalem. He did this in a very short time and in the face of strong opposition. In this way, he gave the small community a respectable defence. But he also inspired them with a renewed sense of unity, identity and purpose.

Ezra was a priest and an expert in the Law of Moses. Along with other experts, he had spent the exile studying and copying the Law. He was very concerned that the new community should live by the law, so that a catastrophe like the exile should never happen again.

He arranged for the Law to be read to all the people, with other priests explaining it as they went along. He organized many reforms among the people and brought them into line with the Law.

In these ways he laid the foundation of what Judaism has been ever since: a community based on and shaped by the Law of Moses.

THE LONG WAIT

And so the period covered by the Old Testament itself came to an end. But it was several centuries before the event it prepared the way for actually happened – the coming of the Messiah.

During those last centuries before Christ, the Jews went through all kinds of experiences. Sometimes they lived more or less at peace. At other times they suffered intense persecution. There was even one period of successful armed independence.

Two things characterized the Jewish people during this time:
● **Devotion to the Law.** After the exile and the time of Ezra, there arose an

God's Servant

Israel was supposed to have been God's obedient servant. As they obeyed God, they would bring knowledge of him to the rest of the nations.

Because Israel had failed, the book of Isaiah speaks of a new figure, who will represent Israel and take on her mission. He is called 'The Servant of God'. There are four special passages which are known as 'The Servant Songs'.

It is worth reading them all at one go. They are: Isaiah 42:1–4; 49:1– 6; 50:4–9 and 52:13— 53:12.

Here are some of the features of this mysterious figure:
● He is obedient to God.
● He will carry out the justice of God.
● He will be filled with God's Spirit.
● He will be a teacher.
● He will suffer and be put to death.
● His death will be for the sake of others.
● He will be exalted after achieving salvation.

It is clear that Jesus was deeply influenced by these prophecies. He saw himself and his own life and death as fulfilling the role of the Servant. It is impossible to read Isaiah 53 without seeing how closely it fits with the experience of Jesus.

'He was oppressed and afflicted, yet he did not open his mouth; he was led like a lamb to the slaughter, and as a sheep before her shearers is silent, so he did not open his mouth.' Isaiah 53:7

almost fanatical desire to keep the Law in every detail. After all, the exile had been God's judgement on his people for disobeying the Law. So they had to be extra careful not to let it happen again.

A special class of experts in the Law grew up. They were known as scribes, rabbis, and (later) the group called the Pharisees. They built around the Law in the scriptures a whole system of additional rules and interpretations. In this way they wanted to make sure that the letter of the Law was kept.

By the time of Jesus this system had become ridiculously overloaded. It was a terrible burden to people who could not keep all the rules. Although Jesus exposed the Pharisees' hypocrisy, we can appreciate the good motives that they had originally.

● **Longing for God's intervention.** Persecution against the Jews increased. The wickedness of the rest of the world seemed to grow unchecked. The Jews

The last book of the Old Testament looks forward to a coming day of the Lord: 'For you who obey me, my saving power will rise on you like the sun and bring healing like the sun's rays.'

began to feel that their only hope lay in direct intervention by God.

This time was filled with hopes and predictions. The Jews longed for the day when God would 'rend the heavens and come down'. They expected that he would bring in his own kingdom. He would destroy the wicked, liberating Israel and put an end to all injustice and suffering.

This was usually associated with a man of destiny who would one day come. He was given a variety of titles among different groups. He was called: Messiah, Elijah, Son of Man, Son of David, the Prophet, and so on. He would lead Israel as their king and bring in the kingdom of God.

This period was a pot that boiled with hopes, mixed in with continuing suffering and disillusionment. So it is not hard to imagine the stirring of heartbeats when John and then Jesus began proclaiming:

'The time is fulfilled! The kingdom of God is at hand! Repent, and believe the gospel!'

📖 PASSAGES TO READ

TUNING IN TO THE NEW TESTAMENT

THE BIBLE'S SECOND HALF

You only need to flick a couple of pages in your Bible to move from Malachi to Matthew. But you are also flicking through centuries of great change and arriving, like a time traveller, in a very different world.

The world is ruled by new imperial masters – the Romans, builders of the greatest and longest-lasting empire the world has ever yet seen. New languages are being spoken. New ideas and customs flood the life of common people. Old hopes are fired by new visions.

A new voice is making itself heard, with a message as old as the old prophets. John the Baptist draws the curtain for the second act of the great biblical drama.

Out of the turmoil of this new age came the New Testament. It is a tiny volume in comparison with the great religious writings of the world's religions – even in comparison with the Old Testament. Yet it has changed the world and its history more than any other religious book.

THE VOICES OF THE NEW TESTAMENT

The New Testament has different ways of speaking to us, though its voices are not quite so varied as those of the Old Testament. There are other important differences to remember, too. The New Testament is much shorter, not only in size (it contains twenty-seven short writings), but also in the length of time involved in producing it. The Old Testament was written over a period of about 1,000 years, spanning many generations. Most of the New Testament was complete within a single generation in the second half of the first century,

'Someone is shouting in the desert, "Prepare a road for the Lord; make a straight path for him to travel!"' Matthew 3:3

within the lifetime of those who were contemporaries of Jesus himself.

Many people think that the Bible speaks a strangely old-fashioned language because they have only heard or read it in the old, authorized, King James Version. It may be a surprise to learn that the New Testament was originally written in a very common, ordinary language indeed.

It was written in Greek – not 'classical' Greek, which was used by writers and playwrights, but 'common' Greek, which was the language of trade and ordinary everyday life. So modern English versions are much nearer to what the writings of the New Testament were originally like.

There are a number of different voices that represent the different kinds of writing in the New Testament.

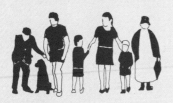

The good news

When, so the story goes, the chief librarian at the ancient university of Alexandria was sent a copy of one of the four Gospels, he was at a loss to know which section of the library it should be placed in.

It was not fiction or drama, because it dealt with a living figure of history. But it was not simply history, because it covered only a short period of time and concentrated solely on one person – Jesus of Nazareth. It was not really biography either. It totally ignored the first thirty years of its subject's life, gave no personal details or descriptions, had very little to say about his family, and gave an extraordinary amount of space to the events of his death.

In the end the librarian decided to open a whole new category – 'Gospel', which simply means 'good news'. It comes from the opening sentence of the book Mark wrote: 'The beginning of the good news about Jesus Christ, the Son of God.'

Documentary

One of the Gospel writers planned a two-volume work. He was Luke, and his first volume was the Gospel that bears his name. But he had also travelled widely with the apostle Paul, and seen the remarkable spread of Christianity. It was a story he believed ought to be told.

He set out to write a detailed account of the main events in the first thirty years of the early Christian church. Luke was a doctor and went about his writing in a careful, methodical way. His book, The Acts of the Apostles, is a well-written historical documentary.

It shows how the Christian faith, starting in Jerusalem, spread throughout Palestine, and then outwards to other Mediterranean lands. Finally it reached Rome, the very centre of the world at that time. Luke's accuracy as a historian has been confirmed at many points from archaeological findings.

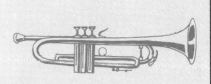

Yours truly...

The earliest writing that found its way into the New Testament, however, was not a Gospel, but a letter. It was the apostle Paul who first used this means of expressing the Christian faith and explaining what it involved in practice. It was a familiar means of communication in his day.

The Romans were great letter writers – in personal, business, political and social life. Paul took over the form, but filled it with Christian content and new kinds of greeting and encouragement. There are twenty-one letters altogether in the New Testament, and thirteen are by Paul. Most of them were written to local church communities in places where Paul had founded the church, or where he had a special interest. A few were written to individuals, and some are general letters – to be read in any church.

But most of the letters were written to people or churches with definite needs and problems. So it is important to find out as much as possible about these details to understand what any letter is about.

The last word

The last book in the Bible is called The Revelation. The book is the only New Testament example of 'apocalyptic' literature (which was mentioned among the voices of the Old Testament).

The Book of Revelation is full of messages and visions given to John to pass on to the Christian churches of his day, who were going through persecution from the state. Its purpose is to show that God is really in control of world events, and that one day he will put an end to the opposition faced by his people.

Revelation is written in highly pictorial and symbolic language. The point of these symbols would have been understood by Christian readers, but not by their pagan persecutors. It is pointless to try to interpret the symbolism literally or to work out elaborate timetables for the end of the world from this book. Its themes are that Christ will return to judge and to reign and that Christians should be ready for that event at all times.

WHY WAS THE NEW TESTAMENT WRITTEN?

Nobody set out to produce something called 'The New Testament'. Nobody said, 'We have an Old Testament; what about writing a New one?' In the early days of Jesus and his apostles, what we now call the Old Testament was referred to simply as 'the scriptures' – literally 'writings'.

Jesus himself wrote nothing down. His last command to his apostles was not that they should go and write a book, but preach the gospel and make disciples. But as they got on with the job of doing just that, all kinds of written material came to be needed for their expanding practical needs. There were three major needs that led to the writing of the New Testament books.

Spreading the message

At first, the work of spreading the message about Jesus was entirely by word of mouth. There was a special emphasis on 'eye-witness' accounts of

Modern printing communicates instant news and opinion. The New Testament writings were rapidly spread around the Roman Empire by the first Christians.

those who had known him during his earthly ministry. That is why the apostles had special status and authority. They were witnesses of what had happened, and they had been authorized and commanded by Jesus to tell what they had seen and heard.

The apostles' preaching and teaching about Jesus soon took on a certain shape. This can be seen from the various records of sermons given by them in the early days of the church. The same features crop up again and again:
● **John the Baptist's preparation.**
● **The ministry of Jesus – his teaching and actions.**
● **The death, resurrection and ascension of Jesus.**
● **The future return of Jesus.**
● **A call to repentance and faith.**

At the same time, it seems that people began to make some written collections of Jesus' sayings, including the Old Testament passages that he was believed to have fulfilled.

While the apostles were alive, all of this could be checked. Anyone's preaching, any church's beliefs, any stories of Jesus or about Jesus that were being told, could be referred to the apostles. They were able to say whether the preaching and stories being told about Jesus were correct. They had authority as eye-witnesses of the events. But as that generation wore on, it became obvious that a permanent written record was needed. This would continue the apostles' authority over the preaching of the church after the apostles themselves had died.

Mark was probably the first to put together a written account, about thirty years after Jesus died. There is good evidence that his main source was Simon Peter, with his rich store of memories. It is a fast-moving account of Jesus, conveying the impact that he made on those who saw and heard him. The other

Gospels were written later, and give different angles on the life of Jesus.

Solving the problems

After Jesus' resurrection, the church grew very quickly. Soon people from different social backgrounds and nationalities were pouring into the church. This led to problems in these young churches:

● **There were questions of belief.** What was the truth about Jesus and the meaning of what he had done?

● **There were questions about behaviour.** How should Christians behave among themselves and in the world?

Sometimes a pressing problem could be settled by a meeting of the church leaders to discuss the matter. When a decision

The questions asked by first-century Christians are common to people of every age. What can we believe? How should we live?

had been reached, an apostle or a delegate could be sent to the problem church to sort things out. This is what happened in Acts 15.

But this could not be done for every problem in a fast-expanding movement. So Paul began the practice of writing letters to churches. Sometimes he wrote to answer specific questions they had sent him. Sometimes he wrote in response to news he had received which disturbed him. In these letters Paul tackles problems to do with belief and behaviour.

Most of Paul's letters were written before the Gospels. So they are the earliest documents we have telling us what Christians believed about Jesus, and how they practised their faith.

These letters carried a very high authority from the start, because they were the words of an apostle of Jesus Christ. That is how Paul carefully describes himself at the opening of his letters and he both wrote and spoke consciously with the authority of Jesus.

> **"**We do not speak in words taught by human wisdom, but in words taught by the Spirit, as we explain spiritual truths to those who have the Spirit. **"**
>
> 1 Corinthians 2:13

As they were copied and circulated to other churches, their authority was accepted by Christians everywhere. They were given the same status as the Old Testament scriptures – that is, writings inspired by God.

Defending the faith

Christianity was not welcome everywhere. Right from the start it met with opposition. Sometimes this opposition was simply violence or persecution. But sometimes it took the form of arguments or propaganda in which the beliefs of Christians about Jesus were denied or twisted. There was a need to set out clear statements of the truth to explain or defend what Christians believed. Some of the books in the New Testament have this as part or all of their purpose.

● There was a need for **defence against hostile Judaism**. This was probably part of the purpose of John's Gospel, and certainly of the letter to the Hebrews.

● There was a need for **defence against false teachers**. They mixed up Christian teachings with elements of Judaism, Greek philosophy and oriental cults. Paul's letters to the Colossians and the Galatians were written to combat such dangerous mixtures.

● There was also a need for **defence against the Roman authorities**. They were suspicious of Christianity because it came from the difficult province of Judea, and also because its founder had made trouble for one of their governors – Pontius Pilate. Part of Luke's purpose in writing Acts was to remove Roman suspicions of Christianity. He showed how Paul had valued his Roman citizenship and had been the victim, not the instigator, of disorder and violence.

So we can see that the writings which make up our New Testament arose out of very practical needs. It is not a cosy book of armchair religion. It was born out of the struggles and pressures in the lives of real people in the real world. Ordinary people, but with an extraordinary message.

PASSAGES TO READ

☐ New Testament Voices

The good news
Mark 1:1–45
The good news
Matthew 1:18—2:23
Documentary
Luke 1:1–38
Documentary
Acts 1:1–26
Yours truly. . .
1 Thessalonians 1:1–10
Yours truly. . .
Philippians 1:1–11
The last word
Revelation 1:1–20

☐ Selections from John

God's Word
John 1:1–51
Jesus' first miracle
John 2:1–25
Conversation with Nicodemus
John 3:1–36
The Samaritan woman
John 4:1–54
The bread of life
John 6:1–71
The light of the world
John 8:1–59
The good shepherd
John 10:1–42

☐ Selections from John

Jesus raises Lazarus
John 11:1–57
Jesus the way
John 14:1–31
Jesus the vine
John 15:1–27
Jesus prays for the disciples
John 17:1–26
Jesus is crucified
John 19:1–42
Resurrection appearances
John 20:1–31
Breakfast with Jesus
John 21:1–25

9

INTRODUCING JESUS

The story of the New Testament is like a fast-moving drama. There are scarcely sixty years between its earliest and latest recorded events, and the bulk of the action is packed into a period of about twenty years. Compared with our leisurely journey through the centuries of the Old Testament, this is like a short sprint. Yet these were the events that changed the world. The New Testament is at the centre of the story of God and mankind.

GET READY!

Mark's Gospel was probably the first to be written. And it opens on a note of dramatic urgency. A voice is shouting. 'Get ready! God is on his way!' It is John the Baptist preparing the way for the main character of the drama to step on stage.

John is like the hinge of the ages. He links together the Old and New Testament, by fulfilling the last great prophecy of Malachi and preparing the way for Jesus himself. Matthew tells us more about John, and about his tragic end. But Mark speeds up the action. Exit John, enter Jesus!

Jesus' opening lines are no less urgent:

❝The right time has come . . . and the Kingdom of God is near! Turn away from your sins and believe the Good News! Mark 1:15 **❞**

This is a summary of his preaching and teaching. It is Jesus and his message in a nutshell. If we can understand what this verse means, it will be a great help in understanding the rest of Jesus' life.

Crisis is the best word to use for the arrival of Jesus. It is a word which originally meant a point of decision, or a turning-point. That is just what Jesus brought.

But it was a double crisis. Jesus announced that something big was happening – and he called on people to do something about it. The gospel of Jesus brought an historical crisis and a personal crisis.

HISTORICAL CRISIS

'The right time has come, the kingdom of God is near.'

These words would have rung loud bells in the ears of Jesus' hearers. Jesus was saying, 'All you have been looking forward to in the future is now here. This is zero hour. The time has come. God is about to act in a new and powerful way.' No wonder excited crowds gathered to hear him and follow him around.

Many, of course, simply would not believe him. Especially those who knew him from his home town. Luke tells us how he tried to explain who he was in Nazareth's synagogue one sabbath day. He said that he was the one who fulfilled the prophecies of the Old Testament. They tried to do away with him there and then, for what they thought was dangerous blasphemy.

But Jesus continued to teach that he was the person sent by God. He was really claiming to be the centre of all human history.

PERSONAL CRISIS

'Turn away from your sins and believe the good news!'

These are the first recorded commands of Jesus. For Jesus was not just declaring facts, he was calling for a response – challenging people to make a decision about what God was doing. Wherever he went people found themselves

confronted with a personal crisis by what he did and said. People were either for him or against him. They could not be neutral about Jesus once they had heard his message and seen what he had done. He told people to do two things: turn and trust.

● **Turn.** Some versions of the Bible use the word 'repent'. But the basic meaning of the word Jesus used was to turn right round and face the opposite direction. Sin has made us turn away from God and

go our own way, so we have to turn away from our sin and let God have control of our lives.

This means that a lot of things are turned upside down. Jesus told many upside down stories. They have shocking and unexpected endings. The things that we often rely on – wealth, ambition – were shown to be useless, or even dangerous.

Look out for examples of this as you read the Gospels. Here are just a few:

The beatitudes (Matthew 5:1–12)
Love your enemies (Matthew 5:43–48)
Like a child (Matthew 18:1–5)
Workers in the vineyard (Matthew 20:1–16)
Losing life and gaining it (Luke 9:23–27)
The rich fool (Luke 12:13–21)
The Pharisee and the tax-collector (Luke 18:9–14)

● **Trust.** Jesus' second command was a call for faith. He asked people to have faith in the good news, which really meant faith in himself, since he was the good news in person. Mark's first chapter immediately goes on to describe such faith in action, when the first disciples obeyed his call to follow him. They soon learned that following Jesus called for total commitment and absolute trust.

He told them that they should refuse to be anxious or worried over the daily necessities of life. If God is put first, he will see to the rest. It is not an easy lesson to learn – then or now. It runs contrary to what we call common sense. We get obsessed with money and possessions because we like to feel secure and provided for. And we live in a world where such things are the dominant concern of most people. But in the midst of such a world, Jesus calls us to live the life of the kingdom of God. That means accepting him as king and then allowing him to be in control.

The kingdom of God

We think of a kingdom as a place, a territory over which a monarch reigns. But that is not the sense of the word as Jesus used it, with its Old Testament background. The 'kingdom of God' is not about a place, but about a person – God ruling as a king.

In the Old Testament

The Jews thought of God's kingship in three ways:
● **God is king over all the earth.** God rules over all people, and not just Israel. Yet not everyone accepts and obeys him as king.
● **God is king over his people, Israel.** Through the covenant, Israel were bound to God as their king. They worshipped him and were supposed to obey him. But even God's own people were imperfect at doing that. So the Jews began to think of God as king in a new way.
● **God will come as king.** God had come to his people in the past, in mighty acts of deliverance. But now the Jewish people looked forward to a future 'Day of the Lord', when he would come and make his kingship clear to all men.

He would purify Israel, defeat their enemies, and reign as king forever. The old age of sin and evil and oppression would end, and there would be a new age of salvation, obedience and peace.

And God would rule over his people through his Messiah. This Messiah would be sent as their deliverer.

What Jesus said

Jesus talked a great deal about the kingdom of God. In his teaching, two main points came across clearly about God's kingdom:
● **It is present in the world now.** The most shocking feature of Jesus' preaching was his urgent insistence that the expected day had dawned. The rule of God was breaking in and people must do something about it in response.

But how was all this happening? In the personality and activity of Jesus himself! Jesus showed how the kingdom of God was present by using word

Jesus said, 'The kingdom of heaven is like this. A man is looking for fine pearls, and when he finds one that is unusually fine, he goes and sells everything he has, and buys that pearl.'
Matthew 13:45–46

pictures and living pictures – his parables and his miracles.

There is a collection of Jesus' parables in Matthew 13. The common idea is that the kingdom of God is something actively at work, even though it may be hidden for a while. It is like seed growing in the ground, or yeast bubbling in dough, or a net gathering fish. It is a living reality in the world now although not everyone may see it.

The followers of John the Baptist once asked Jesus if he really was the Messiah they were all expecting. Jesus replied by pointing to the marvellous works of healing that God was doing through him. The blind could see, the deaf could hear, lepers were healed, lame people were walking, even the dead were being raised to life.

These were exactly the things that Isaiah had prophesied would happen when God came to reign over his people.

The people were looking for other kinds of miracles from the expected Messiah. They wanted to see the miracle of getting rid of the Romans, of Jewish independence. But Jesus knew that the needs of his people were deeper than that.

It was not that God did not care about the injustice and oppression. But Jesus had come to win the victory over sin and evil at its very source – the kingdom of Satan

and the hearts of fallen people.

● It is still to come in its fullness. Christians still pray, 'Your kingdom come'. We still look forward to the day when the kingdom which Jesus began will be completely victorious, and when the whole earth will accept him as king.

Again, the parables of the kingdom in Matthew 13 show this. God's kingdom is like a mustard seed, but it will not stay as a tiny seed. It will grow into the largest of the shrubs. So the kingdom Jesus had brought and begun was only at the start of a long process of growth in the world. There was a lot to be done. The gospel of the kingdom of God had to be preached to all nations on earth before the end would come. That would take time!

So Jesus' preaching of the kingdom of God has this double aspect. It has been present in the world ever since Jesus came. But it will only be completely established when he returns at his second coming. It is important that we understand this double nature, because it lies behind a lot of the teaching in the New Testament. Although Christians continue to live in the midst of this present world, their lives are to be different because of the change that Jesus has already made through his death and resurrection.

Romans, Greeks and Jews

THE ROMANS

At the time of Jesus, the world was Roman. Rome dominates the New Testament. It was a decree of a Roman emperor that brought Joseph and Mary to Bethlehem where Jesus was born. And it was the decision of a Roman governor that ordered his crucifixion.

The Romans made three important contributions to the early history of Christianity:

● **Law and Order.** The Romans had great practical ability in organization. They had a massive structure of law and justice. The strength of this whole framework is shown by its durability. Apart from the 700 years of active Roman rule of most of the Mediterranean lands (and more remote outposts like Britain), the ideals and structures of many Roman institutions survive in modern social systems.

● **Peace and stability.** The peace the Romans brought was not exactly enjoyed by some of the more restless subject peoples – such as the Jews themselves. But it was a fact that in a vast area around the Mediterranean there was a high degree of stability and security. This made it easy to travel from one part of the empire to another.

● **Communications.** The Romans are rightly famous for their roads.

They are a truly amazing achievement. They constructed a network of well-built, almost indestructible roads, as straight as possible, throughout the whole empire. All this was a great help to the early expansion of the church. Apostles and their letters could travel with speed and safety from town to town with the good news of Jesus.

But the New Testament was not dazzled by the glory of Rome. There was the dark side of arrogant imperialism, greed, exploitation and immorality. And the church also experienced severe persecution from several Roman emperors. The Book of Revelation tells us that Rome, like all arrogant human empires will one day be judged and destroyed.

THE GREEKS

The Romans spoke Latin, but the New Testament was written in Greek. Although the world was ruled by Rome, it thought and spoke in Greek.

The Greek contribution to Christianity also has three dimensions:

● **Their language.** Greek was the common language of the civilized world – the language of commerce and literature. It was a language with great richness and with a wide and flexible vocabulary.

Paul preached and wrote in Greek, and could stand up for himself in debate with the intellectuals in Athens itself. Yet at the same time, he could use it to bring the simple power of the message of Jesus to the prostitutes of Corinth.

● **Their contact with Judaism.** Ever since the scattering of Jews out of Palestine by the Assyrians and the Babylonians, many Jewish communities had sprung up around the Mediterranean. Most of these Jewish communities were Greek-speaking and had come under the influence of Greek culture. The old strictness of Judaism was loosened. It was in these communities that Christianity first found it possible to take root.

● **Their failure.** The great philosophers and thinkers of Greece had been brilliant, but they failed to achieve their own highest goals. They longed to find a satisfactory way to understand the universe we live in and to answer the problems of human living. They never did this. The world was ripe for the message of positive hope that Christianity brought.

THE JEWS

The world had a Greek culture and Roman rule, but Jesus was born as a Jew in Palestine. There were a few important groups in Jewish society whose influence we find in the New Testament:

● **The Pharisees.** Their name means 'separate ones'. They believed in preserving the Jewish faith and its customs from the inroads of foreign paganism – especially Greek ways. They believed intensely that the Law of Moses must be kept. In order to make sure people did this, they added a lot of other regulations and followed a very strict way of life. Only Jesus dared to challenge their authority. He exposed the hypocrisy of some of their attitudes and practices.

● **The Sadducees.** The Sadducees were much fewer in number than the Pharisees. They were wealthy aristocrats who controlled the religious establishment. They held on to political power by collaborating with Rome – which made them unpopular. They opposed Jesus and his followers as a political embarrassment to their friendship with the Roman powers.

● **The Zealots.** Some people took their discontent with Roman domination to the point of active violence and resistance. The Zealots hoped for a Messiah who would conquer the Romans. They went in for guerilla and terrorist tactics against the army of occupation.

But as well as all these groups, there were the common people. They heard Jesus gladly, and flocked to him to hear his teaching and to be healed. Some of them were to follow him closely. It was mainly among the ordinary people that Jesus found his closest friends, and from among them that he chose his disciples.

Living with Rome was like living with a tiger. Christians knew that its strength could easily be turned against them. And it was only too easy to become part of its immorality and paganism.

10

WHO IS JESUS?

Jesus provoked questions right from the start of his ministry. In the first chapter of Mark, people were so astonished by his power over evil spirits that they asked each other, 'What is this?' But soon the question changed to 'Who is this?' What kind of man could do what Jesus was doing? That was his disciples' reaction when he calmed the storm: 'Who is this man? Even the wind and the waves obey him.'

The questions continued when he came back to his home town with an exploding reputation for miracles and teaching. 'Where did he get all this?' 'What wisdom is this that has been given him?' 'Isn't he the carpenter, the son of Mary. . .?'

Then Jesus threw in a question of his own, to his disciples:

'Tell me, who do people say I am?' The disciples gave him a briefing on the current assessments. One general view among people was that he was one of the great figures of the past come back to life. John the Baptist. Elijah, or any one of the great prophets.

Then Jesus put the crunch question (which still confronts us today): 'What about you? Who do you say I am?'

Peter came back at once with the answer, 'You are the Messiah'. The disciples still had a lot to learn about the kind of Messiah Jesus was. But it was the turning-point in the disciples' relationship with Jesus. Mark puts it right in the centre of his Gospel. From then on, Jesus taught the disciples in more and more detail about what he had come to do and what was going to happen to him.

So what were the main terms and titles he used about himself?

Three different Gospels

'Why are there four different Gospels?' That is a question that new readers of the Bible sometimes ask. But as we begin to read the Gospels, another question takes its place: 'Why are the first three Gospels so alike?' What point was each one trying to make that made it worthwhile writing a new account?

● **Matthew was probably written for a Jewish Christian community.** He aims to convince his readers that Jesus is the Messiah. So he emphasizes how he fulfilled the Old Testament – even in his birth. And he includes five major teaching sections, showing Jesus to be the great new prophet that was expected.

● **Mark was intended for evangelistic work.** It goes in for urgent, fast-moving action, launching straight into the astonishing life of Jesus. By his miracles, deeds and his authority he is quickly revealed as the Messiah, and then Mark arrives at the key events – the cross and resurrection.

● **Luke wrote mainly for the Gentile world,** especially Romans. He stresses Jesus as King and Saviour, and shows how Jesus brought a radical challenge to the world. He particularly includes Jesus' teaching on the dangers of wealth and power. He also shows an interest in women, in Jesus' prayer life, and in the Holy Spirit.

Pencils scribble, cameras click and whirr as pressmen write their own angle on a story. The Gospels give us different angles on the life of Jesus.

MESSIAH

Messiah is a Hebrew word meaning 'Anointed one'. The Greek word for it is 'Christ'. It refers to someone anointed (specially commissioned) by God to do his work, especially in setting God's people free.

The Judges in the Old Testament were called by God and filled with his Spirit for their tasks of leadership. Later on, when there were kings, they were anointed with oil to symbolize all this. They were 'The Lord's messiahs', his anointed ones.

When the line of reigning kings descended from David came to an end, people began to look to the future, in the hope of a new Messiah. He would be a descendant of David, anointed and empowered by God to be the deliverer of Israel. By the time of Jesus, this messianic hope had become political and nationalistic. They wanted a regal, military leader who would lead them in successful armed rebellion against Rome.

Jesus accepted the title 'Messiah', but he was very cautious about letting it be used. He knew the title would be misunderstood, so he prohibited his disciples from telling others that he was the Messiah. He was right to be cautious. On one occasion the crowd, carried away with messianic enthusiasm, tried to take him by force and make him their king. But Jesus knew his kingdom was not a worldly, political one, though Satan tried to tempt him in that direction.

It was not until after his death and resurrection that his messiahship could be understood properly. Jesus showed his disciples that the Messiah had to suffer before becoming a glorious king. Jesus brought together the idea of Messiah with that of the suffering Servant of the Lord. He was the figure prophesied by Isaiah in the Old Testament.

SON OF MAN

'Son of man' was Jesus' favourite expression when referring to himself. It can be found everywhere in the Gospels, and only Jesus himself used it. So why did Jesus prefer to use this name about himself?

'Son of man' was an Aramaic phrase, from the language Jesus spoke. The phrase could mean 'mankind', or 'a human being', or it could be used as a humble way of speaking about yourself – used instead of 'I' or 'me'. But it also had a meaning that came from Jewish apocalyptic writings, including a passage in Daniel about an exalted person used by God.

Jesus probably chose to use 'Son of man' precisely because it had a double-meaning and would cause questioning. One puzzled group of Jews asked him outright, 'Who is this Son of man?'

By using this expression, Jesus seemed to be saying a number of things about himself:
● **That he was the true representative and leader of Israel.**
● **That he would suffer rejection and death.**
● **That he would rise again in a glorious way.**

This was the claim that enraged the Jewish leaders at his trial. The High Priest asked him if he was the Messiah, and Jesus answered with a claim concerning the Son of man:

❝I am . . . and you will all see the Son of man seated on the right of the Almighty and coming with the clouds of heaven! ❞

Mark 14:62

SON OF GOD

Luke shows us that even as a boy, Jesus was aware of a special relationship with God as his Father. But Jesus only became fully conscious of his identity as the Son of God when John baptized him. On that occasion, the Holy Spirit descended on him (symbolized in the form of a dove), and a voice from heaven gave him the assurance he needed to begin his public ministry: 'You are my own dear Son. I am pleased with you.'

The term came from the Old Testament. There, Israel was called God's son. It was a way of expressing not only the close relationship between God and his people, but also that God expected love and obedience from Israel as his son. The kings of Israel were also known as sons of God – because they were especially called to obey God.

It is this note of faithful obedience which is at the heart of being a son of God. And that was how Jesus thought of his own sonship. He had laid aside his glory and status when he came to earth. Now he would live in total obedience to his Father's will, as the one and only perfect Son of God. Since his baptism, he knew that to do his Father's will would mean suffering. He had come to die.

Jesus, of course, was unique as the Son of God. But there is one feature of his relationship with God as Father which is open to us. Jesus had such an intimate relationship with God that he used an expression that Jewish children use for their own father: 'Abba' – the equivalent of 'Daddy'. Jesus taught his disciples to think of God in this way, too. He taught them what has become the model prayer, known as 'The Lord's Prayer'. And it begins with the familar words, 'Our Father. . .'

LORD

'Lord' was not a term Jesus had used of himself. But it very quickly joined the word 'Messiah' as a popular title for him after his resurrection. This is because it was the only adequate term to express all that Christians found to be true of Jesus. In this way the full title came about which was often used: 'The Lord Jesus Christ'.

The Greek word for 'Lord' was extremely elastic. It could be used as a simple term of respect (like 'sir'), up to the highest title for the Roman Emperor. But more importantly, it was the word used in the Greek translation of the Old Testament to translate the special name of God – Yahweh. So already by the time of Jesus it was in regular use among Greek-speaking Jews as a name for God himself.

So it is significant that the earliest Christians, who were Jews, called Jesus 'Lord', and worshipped him as such. They sang hymns that celebrated him as God. They took passages from the Old Testament that had referred to God and applied them happily to him. The simple sentence, 'Jesus is Lord', is probably the earliest Christian creed, for it sums up the whole of a Christian's faith.

John's Gospel

John's Gospel was almost certainly written later than the other three, and it is very different. John probably knew the first three Gospels, and set out to write an account of Jesus which is much more reflective. **Matthew, Mark and Luke are rather like a series of photographs of Jesus. John's Gospel is more like an artist's portrait.**

He begins in a majestic way by saying that Jesus was the eternal Word of God, who became a real living human person. He then shows how Jesus progressively revealed who he was through his miracles. John calls the miracles 'signs'. They are pointers to his identity.

He then weaves a series of great themes, around certain key words: life and death; light and darkness; truth, love, peace, and so on. In his Gospel, unlike the other three, Jesus is engaged in much lengthier discussions with both his opponents and his friends. He gives five chapters to Jesus' last conversations and prayer with his disciples before his death.

Finally, he explains his purpose in writing, in a word addressed to the reader himself. He wants the reader to believe that Jesus is the Christ, and so come to have eternal life through him. And indeed, it is John's Gospel which is still the most popular in evangelism. It is the Gospel for everyone.

It is John who put the Gospel into the well-known nutshell: 'For God loved the world so much that he gave his only Son, so that everyone who believes in him may not die but have eternal life' (John 3:16).

'I am the light of the world,' Jesus said. 'Whoever follows me will have the light of life and will never walk in darkness.' John 8:12

Jesus said, 'I have come in order that you might have life – life in all its fullness.' John 10:10

Jesus told his followers: 'And now I give you a new commandment: love one another. As I have loved you, so you must love one another. If you have love for one another, then everyone will know that you are my disciples.' John 13:34–35

Jesus' followers were surprised at the close relationship he seemed to enjoy with God. He called God 'Abba' – a word that literally meant 'Daddy'.

PASSAGES TO READ

☐ Selections from Matthew

Baptism and Temptation
Matthew 3:1—4:17
The sermon on the mount
Matthew 5:1–48
First things first
Matthew 6:1–34
Other sayings of Jesus
Matthew 7:1–29
Parables of the kingdom
Matthew 13:24–58
Treating other people
Matthew 18:1–35
Be ready for the future
Matthew 25:1–46

☐ Selections from Luke

Jesus' birth
Luke 2:1–51
Temptation and rejection
Luke 4:1–30
Jesus sends his followers
Luke 9:57—10:42
A lost sheep, coin and son
Luke 15:1–32
Parables and conversations
Luke 18:1–43
Jesus enters Jerusalem
Luke 19:1–48
The Lord is risen indeed!
Luke 24:1–53

Because of who Jesus is. . .

Getting the right answers to the question, 'Who was Jesus?' is not just a matter of interesting fact. It has practical consequences for our faith:

● **God is in control.** Hundreds of years came between the prophecies of the Old Testament and their fulfilment in the New Testament. In that time, people sometimes despaired whether God would ever keep his promises. But he guided history, and all the great empires up to the very moment when the time was right. Then he kept his promise and sent his Messiah. If God can keep his promises on that scale and if he is in control of world history, then we can surely trust him to guide our small circumstances and keep his personal promises.

● **Jesus can be trusted.** When we call Jesus 'the Christ', we acknowledge that he has been anointed by God. That is to say, he was God's choice for our deliverer. He was not some human figure who set himself up as a self-styled deliverer. Still less was he democratically elected as a popular leader! No. It was God who chose, anointed and sent him to be our Saviour. So if we trust in God, we can trust also in Jesus, because he is God's Messiah.

● **Our future is guaranteed.** There are still many great promises about Jesus to be fulfilled. We still look forward to the day when he will reign as Messiah in a new age of peace, over a renewed creation. He promised that we would see him as the Son of man, receiving glory and authority as Judge. Paul looked forward to the day when: 'All beings in heaven, on earth and in the world below will fall on their knees, and all will openly proclaim that Jesus Christ is Lord' (Philippians 2:10–11).

He has promised to those who trust in him that his future is our future. 'Christian' means 'belonging to the Christ'. So one day we will share in all that is his.

● **Christianity can be tested.** Even in New Testament times there were many false beliefs around and Christians had to define what was the true message. They did this by asking who Jesus really was. Only those who would accept that he was the one and only Lord, fully human and yet fully God, were to be regarded as true Christian believers. The same is true today. There are many sects and cults on the fringes of the Christian church. The central test of whether or not they are really Christian is to ask how they regard Jesus. The question, 'Who do you say that I am?' is still as vital today as when it was first asked.

To be a Christian is not just a question of thinking the right things. It means having a new way of life and new reasons for living.

11

ON THE MOVE

'Jesus is the Messiah! Jesus is risen from the dead! We are witnesses of this!' This was the launching-pad of the Christian church. It was a message of tremendous power, for it took the Christian faith, within about thirty years, from its beginnings as an obscure little group of less than 200 people in a corner of Jerusalem to a vast movement numbering hundreds of thousands throughout the civilized world.

This remarkable expansion caught the imagination of Luke, who had himself played a part in it. He was not content to conclude his writing at Jesus' ascension, but carried on to document the main events in those thirty years up to the point where Paul arrived in Rome. Luke's account is known as the Book of Acts.

STARTING IN JERUSALEM

Before Jesus finally left his disciples, he gave them some specific commands:

Stop! in Jerusalem.
Wait! for the gift of the Holy Spirit, as promised.
Go! and be my witnesses throughout the whole earth.

The early church was successful because they obeyed all three commands in the right order. They could have rushed off to the ends of the earth with great enthusiasm, thinking they had all they needed after three years with Jesus. But they waited until they were certain that the Holy Spirit was with them in a powerful way.

In Acts 1–5, Luke describes in careful detail the beginnings of the Christian church. It all began during the Jewish feast of Pentecost, when God poured out his Holy Spirit on the first Christians. The church in Jerusalem had some unmistakable features.

● **The power of the Holy Spirit.** Their experience on the day of Pentecost left them in no doubt that Jesus had kept his promise that they would receive power. Jesus' followers were praying together in the room where the disciples had eaten the Last Supper. Suddenly they heard the sound of a strong wind and saw flames of fire on each others' heads.

Wind and fire had been powerful symbols of God's presence in the Old Testament. Peter, who had denied even knowing Jesus a few weeks earlier, stood up and boldly preached about him to the crowd that had gathered. After this experience, there was no looking back.

The rest of Acts is really 'The Acts of the Holy Spirit', for at every point the Christians were guided and driven forward by him. In this way the gospel was proclaimed and the church exploded on the world.

● **Shared resources.** With breathtaking suddenness, the number of believers leapt from about 120 to over 3,000. What would they all do? Luke's answer to this question is very important, because the Jerusalem church was the model for all future churches. It was the church in all its freshness – born, filled and led by the Holy Spirit.

Above all, Luke emphasizes their community life. These first Christians were not just a collection of individuals who took out membership in a new club. They were a new society, trying to live out their oneness at every level of life.

This expressed itself in four ways:
spiritually (through Holy Communion and prayer);
intellectually (through the apostles' teaching);
socially (through meeting and eating together);
materially (through sharing possessions and eliminating poverty among themselves). Fellowship, for these people, involved their hearts, their heads, their homes, their stomachs and their pockets. It was a totally new commitment of life.

Luke tells us these details in Acts 2. Clearly he wanted to give us the impression that the Christian community life was as important as Peter's words in his sermon. The growth of the church was the result not only of the apostles' preaching, but also of the attractive, practical nature of the church's common social life. This is often stressed elsewhere – especially in Paul's letters to the churches he founded. God's new people are to live a new kind of life.

● **Persecution and expansion.** Very soon the new Christians in Jerusalem ran into opposition from the Jewish authorities. It was hardly surprising. The authorities thought they had just got rid of Jesus, but here were his followers, spreading like wildfire. Worse still, this new movement was a challenge to the established beliefs, patterns and authorities of society, just as Jesus had been.

They were spontaneously solving the problem of poverty by voluntary equality among themselves. They were dissolving the deepest-rooted social barriers – such as race, class, slave or free, male or female. Yet their leaders had no arms or wealth, and no authority, except the 'name of Jesus'. **Most disturbing of all, their loyalty to Jesus was so strong that they would obey no order if they thought it ran against obeying him. It was no good beating or imprisoning them, for they just went on proclaiming Jesus.**

The Christians did not look for political confrontation. But they brought confrontation on themselves because, like Jesus, their life and message were seen as a rebuke and a challenge to the world's way of doing things.

Soon the opposition reached new levels of violence. Stephen was stoned to death. At his trial it was claimed that he had spoken against God, Moses and the temple – similar charges to those brought against Jesus. His death as the first Christian martyr unleashed something of a wave of terror against Jesus' followers in Jerusalem. A man called Saul of Tarsus led the attack. He had witnessed Stephen's death with approval, and hated those whom he thought were uprooting the traditions and beliefs he held so dearly.

But the persecution was like pouring water on an oil fire. It only scattered the flames more widely. Soon the gospel of Jesus had spread beyond Judea. And

Paul carried the message of the Christian faith into the thriving centres of first-century life. These are the ruins of what was once a busy street in Ephesus, the main Roman city in Asia.

Paul the apostle

Paul is the man to whom we owe a major part of the writings in the New Testament. Paul was the all-round first-century man. He was a Roman citizen by his birth in Tarsus. He spoke Greek, but his main sense of personal identity was as a Jew. He was educated in Jerusalem under the famous teacher, Gamaliel, and he became a zealous member of the Pharisees.

When he first came up against the Christians, he hated them with the same intensity as the other Pharisees had hated Jesus himself. He persecuted them fiercely. But right in the middle of this violent persecution, the risen Jesus confronted him and changed his whole life. Paul was immediately convinced that Jesus was the Messiah.

He was baptized by a Christian called Ananias and astounded the believers in Damascus by preaching the same message as theirs. While he was there, he was shown God's purpose for him – that he would be God's agent to bring the Christian gospel to the Gentile world. He also had a foretaste of what it would cost him. He was hounded from Damascus under the threat of death by enraged Jewish opponents.

A period of some years went by before Paul began his travels from Antioch. It was a necessary time of preparation. Paul did a lot of rethinking, and later said that Jesus himself showed him the message he was to preach. That is why he could claim to be an apostle, just like the original disciples, even though he had not known Jesus in his earthly life. He now realized that all the great traditions of his Jewish faith were fulfilled in Jesus, the Messiah. Therefore, the way to God was open for anyone who would trust in Jesus – Jew or Gentile.

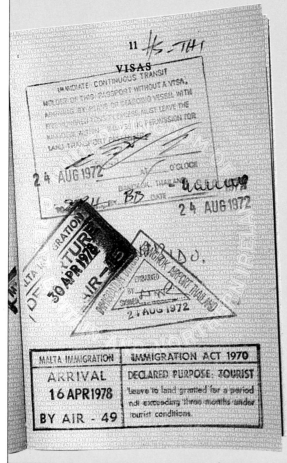

everywhere it had the same powerful effects. So far it had spread solely among Jews, or people with mixed Jewish blood, such as the Samaritans. Then something new and unexpected happened.

GENTILE CHRISTIANS

Peter found himself, to his own surprise, sharing the message of Jesus with non-Jews. And to his even greater surprise, they believed the gospel. The Holy Spirit filled them with the same power as the disciples themselves had experienced at Pentecost.

Peter called for water and baptized the whole household of a Gentile called Cornelius. He argued that if God had so obviously welcomed them, who was he to raise any barrier? And so Gentiles began to be incorporated into the new church. It was a giant step forward.

But it was a step not welcomed by everyone in the church. Peter found himself hauled up before an investigative committee of Jewish Christians. Their Jewish scruples were offended by Peter's association with Gentiles. But when he explained the circumstances, the church gladly accepted that God was giving Gentiles the same opportunity of salvation.

The dispute was not fully settled, and it continued to plague the church for many years. But whatever the arguments, the followers of Jesus were no longer simply a 'sect' within Judaism. They were reaching out to the wider world beyond, in fulfilment of Jesus' own command. The gospel had become international. All of this happened within about ten years of Jesus' death.

THE CHURCH AT ANTIOCH

Antioch was the first truly international church. European Christianity owes its origins to Antioch. Like the Jerusalem church, it had some striking features.

● **Well mixed.** The church there was started by Jewish Christians, but grew also among Greeks and other races. Antioch was a cosmopolitan trade centre, the third largest city in the Roman empire, with a population of half a million. So the Christians would have been even more mixed in class and nationality than Jerusalem. This church demonstrated in its own inner life the meaning of the gospel of reconciliation between people. In fact they were so conspicuous that they attracted the nickname that is still the name of the faith: 'Christians', or 'Christ-people'.

● **Well taught.** First they had Barnabas. Then he fetched Saul of Tarsus (now converted and known as Paul), who was proving his gifts as a teacher and preacher. Between them they gave the church a whole year of solid teaching. It is no accident that such sound teaching led the church to send people hundreds of miles to preach the message of Jesus. Once they had grasped the truths of the Christian faith, they saw the needs of the world more clearly.

● **Well led.** The Christians at Antioch did not depend completely on Saul and Barnabas for their leadership. This church was far from being the one-man band that some are. It had a team of leaders who were prophets and teachers. They too were mixed. One of them, Simon called Niger, was probably black, as 'Niger' is Latin for black. They were spiritual and prayerful, and acted decisively once they knew what God wanted.

● **Generous.** When there was a famine in Judea, they responded as soon as they became aware of it. Everybody worked to provide a gift for the Christians in Judea, and the leaders themselves delivered it. It was a tangible proof of genuine Christian unity between the Gentile Christians of Antioch and the Jewish Christians of Jerusalem.

● **Outward looking.** They were willing to receive outsiders (Barnabas and Paul) to meet their own needs at one time. But then they were willing to give them away again to meet the needs of others. They did this when they sent Paul and Barnabas out on their first journey to preach in other countries. Then they made sure that they received them back, with keen interest in what God was doing in other parts of the world.

All these features mark Antioch as a prophetic church. A prophet is someone who is in tune with two things: in tune with God and with the world around. At Antioch, they listened to what God was saying, and they were aware of real needs in the outside world. They knew Jesus, and they knew the world, and they brought the two together.

Because of this, Antioch became the place where a Jewish-based faith was able to mature and become a truly world-wide faith.

PAUL THE TRAVELLER

It was about AD46 when the Christians of Antioch commissioned Paul and Barnabas for the work the Holy Spirit wanted them to do. For Paul it meant twenty years of almost continual travelling. The longest time he spent in any one place was just over two years. And in those years he endured every kind of physical hardship, along with emotional and spiritual pressures. His account in 2 Corinthians 11:24–28 makes grim reading:

'Five times I was given the thirty-nine lashes by the Jews; three times I was whipped by the Romans; and once I was stoned. I have been in three shipwrecks, and once I spent twenty-four hours in the water. In my many travels I have been in danger from floods and from robbers, in danger from fellow-Jews and from Gentiles; there have been dangers in the cities, dangers in the wilds, dangers on the high seas, and dangers from false friends.

'There has been work and toil; often I have gone without sleep; I have been hungry and thirsty; I have often been without enough food, shelter or clothing. And not to mention other things, every day I am under the pressure of my concern for all the churches. . .'

● **The first journey** (Acts 13–14). After visiting Cyprus, Paul, Barnabas and John Mark (who later wrote Mark's Gospel), arrived on the coast of Pamphylia (now southern Turkey). Mark returned home, but Paul and Barnabas went on to preach in several cities.

Their plan of attack was to go first to the Jewish synagogues and preach Jesus as the Messiah. Only after that would they preach to the Gentile outsiders. They met with considerable success and churches were founded in each town. But opposition was also fierce and Paul was stoned almost to death in one place.

They returned to Antioch by the same route, encouraging the new believers and appointing leaders for them. Back in Antioch, they told the Christians how God had opened up these new towns to the gospel, bringing to birth little churches just like Antioch – mixtures of Jews and Gentiles, now united in their faith in Jesus.

● **The second journey** (Acts 15:36–18:22). This further influx of Gentile believers into the church brought an old controversy to the boil. Some Jewish Christians from Jerusalem insisted that Gentile Christians should be circumcised and keep the Jewish Law as well as believing in Jesus. This led to a major meeting of the apostiles and church leaders in Jerusalem. Luke gives a full account of the proceedings in Acts 15. They decided that there was no need for Gentile Christians to be bound by the Jewish laws and customs. Faith in Jesus Christ was all that was necessary for salvation.

Paul wanted to let his new churches know about this decision. So he set off on a second journey, this time taking with him a new companion, Silas. After revisiting the towns of his first journey, and picking up young Timothy as another trusted companion, he turned north-west and arrived at Troas on the coast. There God gave him a dream of a man from Greece asking him to come over and help them there. At this point Luke himself must have joined Paul in his travels, for his story changes from 'them' to 'us' at Acts 16:10.

So the tiny group arrived in Greece, and with them the gospel arrived in Europe. Again they followed the same policy of going to the Jewish community first, and then, when they rejected or opposed the message, taking it to the Gentile population.

Paul was forced to keep moving as much by violent opposition as by his own desire to take the gospel where it had not yet been heard. But he left behind churches which remained stable and strongly supportive of him in the rest of his travels. He had special links with the churches at Philippi and Thessalonica. This can be seen from his letters to them.

● **The third journey** (Acts 18:23–21:16). This time, Paul made straight for Ephesus. It was the major city in the important Roman province of Asia. Paul saw that it was strategic for the spread of the gospel in that part of the world. So he stayed there more than two years, teaching and lecturing in a hired public hall. In this way the church was firmly established and spread to surrounding towns in the province. This was possibly one of the most fruitful periods of his ministry.

It was also at this time that he wrote letters to the church in Corinth. But Paul was forced to leave Ephesus. The pagan metal-workers were losing their trade in idol images because of the growth of the Christian church. There was a serious riot, and Paul was driven out.

He went back to the Greek mainland, revisiting his churches and collecting the gift that he planned to take to the impoverished churches in Judea. While in Corinth he wrote his letter to the Christians in Rome, whom he had not met, but hoped to visit on a later trip.

Romans is Paul's most careful and systematic presentation of the gospel he preached and taught. Then he returned to Palestine, and eventually reached Jerusalem itself.

PAUL THE PRISONER

The final chapters of Acts are taken up with Paul's arrest in Jerusalem and his journey to Rome. Paul spent the next four or five years as a prisoner of the Romans. First of all he was held in Jerusalem and Caesarea. And after a terrifying and exhausting sea journey, he was held in Rome.

He was put under a kind of house arrest, rather than proper imprisonment. Every time he was given an opportunity to defend himself, he used it to speak up for Jesus instead. And in Rome, he continued to do the same for the two

years he awaited trial. During this time he wrote his letters to the Ephesians and the Colossians.

That is where Luke brings his two-volume work to a close. He began with Jesus proclaiming the kingdom of God in the remote lakeside villages of Galilee. And he finishes with Paul doing the same in the heart of the capital of the world:

❝For two years Paul lived in a place he rented for himself, and there he welcomed all who came to see him. He preached about the Kingdom of God and taught about the Lord Jesus Christ, speaking with all boldness and freedom. Acts 28:30–31 **❞**

PASSAGES TO READ

☐ The Message Spreads	☐ Selections from Romans	☐ Paul's Travels
The day of pentecost *Acts 2:1–47*	**Mankind's guilt** *Romans 1:1–32*	**Paul's first journey** *Acts 13:1–3, 49—14:28*
Peter and John arrested *Acts 4:1–37*	**God's judgement** *Romans 2:1–29*	**Paul's second journey** *Acts 15:36—16:40*
Stephen's death *Acts 6:1–15; 7:51–60*	**God's solution to our sin** *Romans 3:1–31*	**Athens and Corinth** *Acts 17:16—18:11*
The message spreads *Acts 8:1–40*	**Right with God** *Romans 5:1–21*	**Paul's third journey** *Acts 20:1–38*
Saul meets Jesus *Acts 9:1–43*	**Slaves of God** *Romans 6:1–23*	**Paul appeals to the Emperor** *Acts 25:1–27*
Peter and Cornelius *Acts 10:1–48*	**Struggling to do good** *Romans 7:1–25*	**Perilous voyage to Rome** *Acts 27:1–44*
Peter freed from prison *Acts 12:1–25*	**God's Spirit** *Romans 8:1–39*	**Paul in Rome** *Acts 28:1–31*

12

UNDER PRESSURE

Conflict concentrates the mind wonderfully. Especially if it is violent. If you are going to be stoned, lynched or thrown in prison for what you believe, then you will want to be absolutely clear about what it is you do believe and why.

Most of the letters in the New Testament were written to Christians facing one form of conflict or another – sometimes physical persecution, sometimes a conflict of ideas which threatened the truth of the gospel. Paul and the other New Testament writers were forced to argue for the key truths of the Christian faith.

CONFLICT WITH FALSE TEACHINGS

The message of Jesus had to struggle for survival in a world full of pagan ideas and philosophies. But the issues were not always clear-cut. The most dangerous situations arose when pagan ideas were mixed in with Christian teaching, and borrowed Christian words.

The battlefields

There are three groups of letters in which Paul is concerned about the effects of false teaching in his churches:

● **Corinthians.** There were divisions and quarrels in the church at Corinth. Some people took great pride in their spiritual wisdom, which was really very immature. There were also sexual immorality and problems over marriage. Not to mention confusion over the resurrection.

Paul dealt with these problems in the two letters we have out of the four he actually wrote to them. He also had to give a lot of space in these letters to defending his own authority as an apostle, commissioned by Jesus to teach the truth and expose the error of the false teachings.

● **Colossians and Ephesians.** Paul wrote these two letters at the same time, while he was under house arrest in Rome. He had never personally visited the church at Colossae. But he felt responsible for it, since it had been founded by people converted during Paul's time in Ephesus. So there are many similarities between the letters. It was the Colossian church that worried Paul most. The false ideas and beliefs had infected it badly. His letter to them is a brilliant counter-attack.

Paul's method of dealing with this batch of false beliefs was not to argue over the tiny details, as he tended to do with his Jewish opponents. Instead he set out to present the greatness and glory of Christ in such a positive and exalted way that these other ideas are made to look like what they really are – 'empty deceit'. He explains how Jesus Christ is superior to all the powers and spirits of the false teachers. His own words cannot be bettered:

❝Christ is the visible likeness of the invisible God. He is the first-born Son, superior to all created things. For through him God created everything in heaven and on earth, the seen and the unseen things, including spiritual powers, lords, rulers, and authorities. God created the whole universe through him and for him. Colossians 1:15–16 **❞**

● **Timothy and Titus.** These were the last letters of Paul's life. He wrote them because he was concerned about the younger men he had left in charge of some of his churches. There is the same concern in all of them that Timothy and Titus should not allow their churches to be led astray by false teachings, silly arguments and speculation. They should hold fast to the sound teaching Paul had given them, and pass it on to other teachers.

When the smoke cleared

In a way, the false teachings faced by Paul were valuable to the growth of the New Testament. They made Paul and the other writers state very clearly exactly what the gospel was, and what it definitely was not. As Paul crossed swords with his opponents, the Christian gospel was sharpened. Several New Testament beliefs stand out strongly because of these clashes:
● **The uniqueness of Christ.** Jesus

As in any construction, team work was essential in building up the churches that Paul helped to start. They had to work together to overcome the difficulties they faced.

Law and freedom

The conflict with the Jews was the most tragic conflict of all. Jesus himself was a Jew, as were the apostles and most of the Christians in the first decade of the church's life. Jesus came as the Messiah, and so faith in him should have been the natural outcome of the ancient faith of Judaism. This conflict took two forms:

● **Those who rejected the claim that Jesus was the Messiah** opposed and attacked his followers.

● **Jewish Christians who could not accept any loosening of their Jewish customs and beliefs** alongside their faith in Jesus. This made them very unhappy at the way the apostles were handling the mission to the Gentiles. It was just not right, they thought, that a pagan Gentile could become a Christian just like that.

These Jewish Christians caused a dispute at Antioch. Later they followed Paul and tried to make his churches submit to Judaism. Some of them were ex-Pharisees. But Paul called them 'Judaizers'.

Paul's reply

Paul's main point was that salvation depended on Jesus alone. To add anything else was to take away from what Jesus had done. He argues this most clearly in Romans 1–8:

● **All have sinned.** Jews have their written Law, but they break it. Gentiles have no written law, but they sin against what they know of God's law in their consciences. So although the Jews have had greater privileges, both are equally guilty in the sight of God. And there is no way any of us can rub out the fact of our sin by any amount of doing good.

● **Christ died for everyone.** When Jesus died on the cross, he was being punished for the sins of all people. So forgiveness is available to all who trust in him, regardless of race or background.

● **God puts us right.** Getting right with God is not something we can do for ourselves. It is something God does for us. God takes away our sins because Jesus has already paid the penalty for them. So as we trust in Jesus, God pardons us. He declares us not guilty. There is no longer any accusation against us.

● **This is a gift.** Being put right with God is not something we can earn or deserve. Keeping the Law of Moses or doing good is not enough. It is a gift from God, which we simply accept by faith when we trust in Jesus. This is the only way for both Jews and Gentiles to be put right with God, and to be made friends with each other.

Why Paul said it

It is very important that we see that this was not

just some tedious dispute between ex-Pharisees over ancient customs. If it had been, Paul would never have got involved with it. He fought so adamantly over this issue because he saw that three vital things were at stake in it. His letter to the **Galatians** spells this out:

● **Christ's glory.** The Judaizers agreed that Jesus was the Messiah. But they failed to see that his coming had ended the old age of the Law. Jesus was now the only way to God. And they failed to see that by dying and rising, Jesus had done all that was needed for us to be put right with God.

● **Mankind's salvation.** Paul saw clearly that if Jesus was the only way to be put right with God, then people would not be saved and forgiven if they tried any other way. They could only come to know God by knowing the truth of the gospel. Anyone who obscured that truth must be opposed, for their own good.

● **Christian freedom.** As long as people imagine that they have to earn the right to God's favour by doing good,

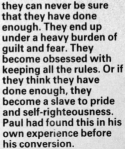

they can never be sure that they have done enough. They end up under a heavy burden of guilt and fear. They become obsessed with keeping all the rules. Or if they think they have done enough, they become a slave to pride and self-righteousness. Paul had found this in his own experience before his conversion.

But it was a bondage from which Christ had set him free. He now knew that God puts us right with himself from his side. And so he preached this wonderful freedom to the Gentiles, who experienced and enjoyed it.

Christ is not just the leader of a Jewish sect. Still less is he one among many spirits or angels between God and humanity. He is Lord of all creation – earthly and heavenly. He is Lord of all history, past, present and future. He is Lord of his whole church, and Lord of the individual Christian.

● **The humanity of Christ.** Jesus was fully human. He had not been a man pretending to be God, or God pretending to be a man, but fully both. And as a man he had died on the cross for us. The New Testament makes the fact that God became fully human in Jesus a test of genuine Christianity.

● **The mystery of Christ.** The false teachers loved to talk about mysteries. They thought of mysteries as secret knowledge that only the privileged few were initiated into. Paul, too, loved to speak of the 'mystery of Christ'. But for him it was a completely open secret which God had made available to all people through the preaching of the apostles. It was the truth that through Jesus the way to God was open for anyone.

The false teachers

What did these false teachers say, and what effect did they have?

● **Their teachings.** They said that there was an infinite gulf between God and the physical universe, including mankind. God was spiritual and holy, but everything material or physical (including our human bodies) was utterly evil. Obviously, this is a direct contradiction of the Old Testament teaching on creation. They also refused to believe that God could have had any part in human history, since it was so evil. That too was a rejection of the Old Testament.

For the same reasons, they misunderstood Jesus. They gave no importance to his historical life and death. And he could not have been God in human form, because physical flesh was evil. They said that Jesus could not be the one true way to God as he and his apostles claimed. Instead, they filled up the gulf between God and mankind with an infinite host of spirits and powers. Jesus was just one of these powers to help people get to God.

The only way people could reach God was for their souls to rise through the ranks of these spiritual beings, by an ever increasing process of knowledge and enlightenment. This meant they had no place either for the bodily resurrection of Jesus Christ, or for the future hope of resurrection for Christians.

● **Their effects.** These false beliefs had no place for sincere repentance. Instead they went to one or other of two extremes. Either they went in for a very negative type of self-denial. They refused certain foods, avoided marriage, and observed special rituals. Or they went in for gross immorality. They said that if your soul was saved by this special knowledge, then it didn't matter what you did with your physical body! It was evil anyway, so why not?

These beliefs were extremely dangerous. They could easily have swallowed up the true gospel and left the Christian church as nothing more than yet another failed first-century cult. But thanks to Paul and his concern for his young churches, that did not happen.

CONFLICT WITH AN IMMORAL WORLD

In all the churches, another important conflict was going on all the time. It involved every Christian. It was a conflict over life itself. How should a Christian live? The great majority of early Christians were ordinary people, from pagan backgrounds, living and working among pagan friends, and surrounded by all the superstitions and customs of the time. The big question that faced them every day was, 'What practical difference does it make to daily living now that I am a believer in Jesus Christ?'

Paul never started by telling his readers how they should live. He assumed that his readers were Christians, and that they had experienced new life through Jesus. This was where he started.

He said that there is no point in trying to live as you think a Christian should unless you have already become a Christian. Without that new life inside, there can be no new lifestyle on the outside.

But there is another side to this coin. If we have experienced this new life, then it must show itself in practical Christian living.

Togetherness

The challenge and conflict of Christian living in a pagan world was not something that Paul expected the individual Christian to sort out for himself or herself. Modern people sometimes mistakenly think this. 'Religion is a private thing,' they say; 'I keep myself to myself.' But that is not the way of the New Testament life at all.

Jesus gathered together a small

The Christian life is a life of growth. Paul talked about the Holy Spirit as the one who gives new life and helps us to grow like Jesus.

Living in the real world

Hebrews

The letter to the Hebrews tackles the same questions that Paul answered. Should Christians still obey all the Old Testament laws and customs? Hebrews was written to Jewish Christians under the pressure of persecution, who were tempted to go back to their former life in Judaism.

The writer argues in detail that Jesus as God's Son has fulfilled all the great features of the Old Testament faith: Moses, the covenant, the priests, the sacrifices and the temple. He was the new and better way to God. And he had brought a new covenant that would never be replaced.

The book is full of encouragements to stand firm, and it rings with the assurance that God's promises are reliable. It also shows that you cannot understand the New Testament properly without some knowledge of the Old Testament!

James

James' letter is a practical one, dealing with down-to-earth Christian living. His letter is written to challenge people who are 'double-minded', believing one thing but acting in a quite different way. James attacks this way of living on a number of fronts:

● **Hearing and doing.** It is easy to listen to God, but much harder to change as he wants us to. Hearing and doing must work together (chapter 1).

● **Faith and actions.** 'Faith by itself,' says James, 'if it is not accompanied by action, is dead' (chapter 2). We must do what we believe.

● **Praising and cursing.** A boat is steered by a small rudder. In the same way, our lives are steered by our tongues. What we say reflects what we are inside. A double-minded person will praise God, but curse other people (chapter 3).

● **God and the world.** Some people like to be on friendly terms with both God and the world. But in chapter 4 James says we must choose between the two. This sums up the message of James. God wants people who are single-minded in their determination to follow him.

1 Peter

The letter of 1 Peter was written to people who were suffering because of their Christian faith. Peter wrote to encourage them in a number of ways. He said that:

● The resurrection of Jesus gives us a hope that cannot be destroyed – even by death.

● The suffering we endure now proves that our faith in God is genuine. When faith is under fire then we discover its true strength.

● Suffering also makes us choose for or against the Christian faith. Peter encouraged his readers to live for God fully, not in a half-hearted way.

Peter stresses again and again in his letter the joy of being a follower of Jesus. He says that Christians together are like the stones in a building used to worship God:

'Come to the Lord, the living stone rejected by man as worthless but chosen by God as valuable. Come as living stones, and let yourselves be used in building the spiritual temple. . .' 1 Peter 2:4–5

1 John

John's letter was written to combat two dangerous ideas. False teachers were spreading around the idea that Jesus had not been a real human being. And they also said that Christians could live as they liked – morality didn't matter at all.

John writes clearly and powerfully against these false ideas. He says that Jesus was fully a human being – the first disciples had heard, seen and touched him for themselves. And he stresses that God is concerned for the way that Christians behave. Those who say that they love God must show it by their love and concern for each other.

'This is the message we have heard from him and declare to you: God is light; in him there is no darkness at all. If we claim to have fellowship with him yet walk in the darkness, we lie and do not live by the truth. But if we walk in the light, as he is in the light, we have fellowship with one another, and the blood of Jesus, his Son, purifies us from every sin.' 1 John 1:5–7

community of those who had responded to his teaching about the kingdom of God. And he showed them that together they must live by the standards of the kingdom of God in contrast to the ways of the world. This new way of life worked out in different ways:

● **Living together.** If any group of human beings decide to share their lives and interests, a whole range of potential problems lies in store: difficult relationships, petty jealousies and rivalries, personality clashes, and so on. Jesus' disciples displayed them all in their close life together. How were they to overcome these problems?

Jesus had given his disciples the key in his great command, 'Love one another, as I have loved you.' But it was Paul who spelt out what that means in practical detail.

For Paul, the essence of love was the determination to seek the good of the other person. It meant putting his needs and interests before yourself. That was exactly what Jesus Christ had done, and it was the only pattern for Christians to follow in their life together.

● **Worshipping together.** Paul also regarded the worshipping life of the local church as a vital ingredient in strengthening Christians for their moral struggle in the world. In Ephesians and Colossians he includes worship right in the middle of his teaching about practical Christian living. There are two reasons for this.

First, you can only worship God in a way that pleases him if your daily life pleases him. And second, it is in worship that the Christian family meets with the living Christ. By meeting with him we can be challenged, comforted and strengthened by him. He sends us out into the world again to live as he wants us to.

● **Learning together.** Paul expected his readers to be learning regularly. He knew that this was an important way for Christian morality to be built up. He saw that the biggest reason for the Corinthian church's problems with immorality was that they were so immature in their thinking.

Almost all his letters include a prayer that his readers would grow in their knowledge and wisdom. Then they would be able to know how to live in a way that pleases God. This was not a question of being academic or intellectual. Paul wanted Christians to have renewed minds, so that they would live renewed lives.

CONFLICT WITH PERSECUTION

Official state persecution of Christians did not become a serious threat until the end of the century in which the New Testament was written. But right from the beginning, Christians faced opposition and hostility from both Judaism and paganism. To go on living under that kind of pressure, they needed to be confident that what they believed and proclaimed was really true. But how could they be sure?

Certainty for the present

Suppose you asked an average first-century Christian, 'How can you be so sure that your sins are forgiven, that you are safe from God's judgement and really belong to God's people?' He might answer by first of all talking about Jesus – how he was God's Messiah, how he had risen and ascended as Lord and yet was still present with his followers.

If you then asked him how he knew all that, he would probably point out how he had been taught it all. People who had actually known Jesus and had seen him alive again after his death had told him about it.

But suppose you pressed him further about how he could be so sure about all this. In the end he might well simply reply, 'Because I just know! Deep down inside, I have this complete certainty that I am a child of God, because Jesus Christ, God's Son, has saved me from my sin and I belong to him.'

That inner certainty is the work of the Holy Spirit. It is his speciality. And it is the right and privilege of every Christian, because every Christian has received the gift of the Holy Spirit. The Holy Spirit is not an impersonal force, but the presence and power of Jesus. When we talk about him, we are talking about God at work as a person. But how does he work? The New Testament gives us some pointers:

● **A seal.** In the ancient world, a seal was used for several purposes. It could prove ownership of something: The Holy Spirit assures a Christian that he or she belongs to God. Or it could prove something was genuine, like the hallmark on a gold or silver object: the presence of the Holy Spirit proves the genuineness of a Christian's faith.

● **A deposit,** or down-payment, secures a purchase, by guaranteeing that the rest of the payment will be made in due course. God has given us the Holy Spirit, with all the blessings he brings, as the first instalment of all that he promises for our future (Ephesians 1:14). So the Holy Spirit brings into the present a foretaste of the blessings of heaven itself – peace, joy, love, harmony and wholeness.

● **He tells us that we are sons of God.** The Holy Spirit assured Jesus at his baptism that he was God's Son. And he makes us realize that God is our Father. He gives us confidence to trust him, talk to him, and know that we can never be separated from him (Galatians 4:6–7).

● **He makes us more like Jesus.** This is God's whole purpose in making us his children, and it is the practical hallmark of genuine Christian faith. Of course, becoming more and more like Jesus is something we can never do by our own effort, just by keeping a lot of rules. It is only something the Holy Spirit can do, as he lives in us and produces his own fruit in our lives (Galatians 5:22–25). As he does so, we grow in our certainty that God really is in control of our lives.

A living hope

The apostles were absolutely sure of the fact of the resurrection because they had seen Jesus, risen and alive. They were equally sure that he would come back again, to bring to an end the evil age of this world and to establish his own eternal kingdom. They were sure of this because Jesus himself had promised to return.

Paul pictures the return of Jesus happening with a great blast on a trumpet! That trumpet sends its notes back through time to the life of Christians in the present.

● **A note of encouragement.** The knowledge that Jesus would return was a great comfort for the bereaved, and it still is. Paul pointed this out to Christian believers at Thessalonica who mourned for Christians who had died. The return of Jesus is also used to strengthen those who face persecution – which is the major purpose of the Book of Revelation.

● **A note of urgency.** The New Testament writers take the line: 'Since we believe Jesus will return, let's make sure we live as he wants us to.' Jesus had made the same point in some of his parables. There is an emphasis on taking life seriously, and getting on with the work God has given us. We are told to remember that the time available to us is limited. We don't want to be ashamed at having to face Jesus when he returns.

● **A note of joy.** When Paul and others speak of hope, they do not mean a fragile wish that may be disappointed, but the certainty of faith that Jesus will keep his promise. And so this hope is always accompanied by exuberant joy. The Christian's joy is indestructible, because his past is wiped clean by God's forgiveness, his present is filled with God's presence, and his future means seeing Jesus for himself. No wonder Peter called it 'a great and glorious joy which words cannot express!'

The ultimate event

What will it be like when Jesus comes back? Although it is beyond our imagination, the New Testament does give us some details. They can be found in Mark 13:24–37, 1 Thessalonians 4:13–18 and Revelation 20:11—21:27.

● **Personal.** Jesus will come in person. It will not just be his 'influence'. It will be recognizably Jesus himself.

● **Public.** The second coming will be seen by all mankind. The disciples saw him ascend, and the angels promised a similar, visible return. The favourite New Testament word for the event was also used for the public arrival of a king or important ruler in a town, with great splendour and spectacle.

● **Unexpected.** Jesus warned that it would be as sudden as lightning, as unexpected as a thief in the night. He said that the actual date was not known even by him, but only by the Father. So we are to be ready at all times. Our job is to prepare for it, not to waste time trying to predict it.

● **In glory.** At his first coming, Jesus came in humility, danger and poverty – and he was rejected by people. His second coming will be a magnificent kingly event, with the heavenly hosts that serve him as king. He will then establish for ever the kingdom he began, and be accepted as Lord by everyone.

● **In judgement.** Jesus will not come, as he did before, to be judged by people, but rather he will come to execute God's judgement on us.

● **A new creation.** The return of Jesus will bring to an end the present world order, with all its twisted corruption, evil and frustration. But that destruction will not be God's last word on his creation. He will create a new creation, in which he will once again live with his people. Christians do not look forward to living as souls in heaven, but to life in resurrected bodies, with Jesus Christ, in God's new creation.

PASSAGES TO READ

☐ James and Peter

Practical wisdom
James 1:1–27
Believing and doing
James 2:1–26
Taming the tongue
James 3:1–18
Rely on God
James 4:13—5:20
Living to please God
1 Peter 1:1—2:10
Christian suffering
1 Peter 2:11—3:22
Be alert!
1 Peter 4:1—5:14

☐ John and Hebrews

Love one another
1 John 1:1—3:3
God is love
1 John 4:7—5:21
God's Son is the greatest
Hebrews 1:1—2:4
Jesus the High Priest
Hebrews 3:1—4:16
Christ's sacrifice
Hebrews 10:1–25
Living examples of faith
Hebrews 11:1—12:11
Keep on the way
Hebrews 13:1–21

☐ A Hope for Living

Altered lives
Ephesians 4:1–32
Living as God's children
Ephesians 5:1–33
God's armour
Ephesians 6:1–24
Messages to the churches
Revelation 2:1–29
Messages to the churches
Revelation 3:1–22
A new creation
Revelation 21:1–27
Come, Lord Jesus!
Revelation 22:1–21

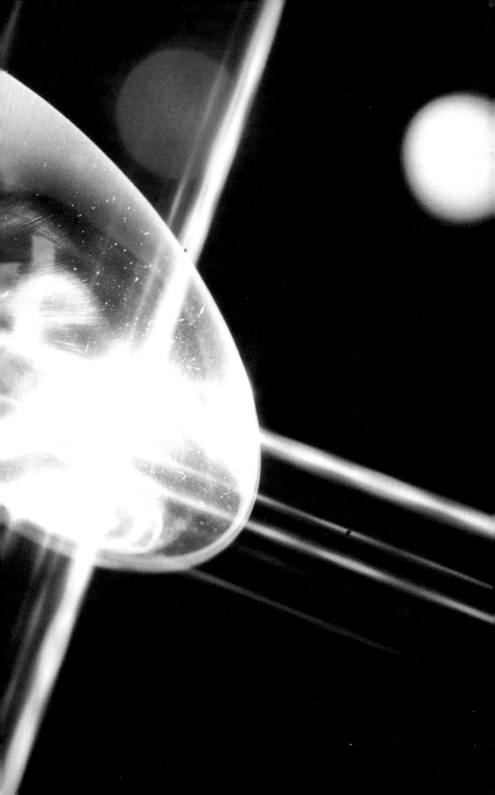